D1083365

FUSION

LEADERSHIP

FUSION
LEADERSHIP

UNLEASHING THE MOVEMENT OF
MONDAY MORNING **ENTHUSIASTS**

DUDLEY R. SLATER
WITH STEVEN T. TAYLOR

GREENLEAF
BOOK GROUP PRESS

This publication is designed to provide accurate and authoritative information in regard to the subject matter covered. It is sold with the understanding that the publisher and author are not engaged in rendering legal, accounting, or other professional services. If legal advice or other expert assistance is required, the services of a competent professional should be sought. The names and identifying characteristics of certain individuals in this book have been changed to protect their privacy.

Published by Greenleaf Book Group Press
Austin, Texas
www.gbgpress.com

Copyright ©2017 Dudley R. Slater and Steven T. Taylor

Distributed by Greenleaf Book Group

For ordering information or special discounts for bulk purchases, please contact Greenleaf Book Group at PO Box 91869, Austin, TX 78709, 512.891.6100.

Design and composition by Greenleaf Book Group and Sheila Parr
Cover design by Greenleaf Book Group and Sheila Parr
Cover image ©CoolKengzz / Shutterstock

For permission to reproduce copyrighted material, grateful acknowledgment is made to the Greenleaf Center for Servant Leadership.

Edited by Cindy Collins-Taylor

Cataloging-in-Publication data is available.

Print ISBN: 978-1-62634-401-3

eBook ISBN: 978-1-62634-402-0

Part of the Tree Neutral® program, which offsets the number of trees consumed in the production and printing of this book by taking proactive steps, such as planting trees in direct proportion to the number of trees used: www.treeneutral.com

TreeNeutral®

Printed in the United States of America on acid-free paper

17 18 19 20 21 22   10 9 8 7 6 5 4 3 2 1

First Edition

To Jim, Trent, Goose, Matt, Mark, Jason, Carol, Ken, Steve, Byron, Mike, Lisa, Deb, Matt, Dean, John, Dave, Julie, Jeff, Chris, and our 2,337 other team members, the greatest team to serve our industry.

And to Laurie, Toryn, and Kathrina, the greatest team to grace my life.

CONTENTS

ON AND OFF THE COURT: FUSION LEADERSHIP PRINCIPLES IN ACTION

by Terry Porter

A two-time NBA all-star who played professional basketball for seventeen years and coached in the league for many more, Terry Porter is currently the head coach at the University of Portland, in Oregon. He's also known throughout the Portland area and nationally for his work with charities and his community service.

When I was asked to write the foreword to *Fusion Leadership: Unleashing the Movement of Monday Morning Enthusiasts*, I quickly accepted the invitation. I think I know a thing or two about leadership, because I've been fortunate to have learned from so many great leaders. They taught me valuable lessons about how to succeed, lead, motivate others, contribute to and achieve a common mission, give back to your community, and live a full and meaningful life.

I took a little something from each of the wonderful coaches I had during my career: Dick Bennett, who coached me at the

University of Wisconsin–Stevens Point, Jack Ramsay and Rick Adelman with the Portland Trail Blazers, Flip Saunders with the Minnesota Timberwolves, Pat Riley with the Miami Heat, and Gregg Popovich with the San Antonio Spurs.

And you know what? In their own way, each of these coaches deployed at least one of the tools outlined in this book. As I read *Fusion Leadership*, I realized, time after time, that my own leadership style closely aligns with the principles, techniques, and values that compose the Fusion Leadership model. Like Dudley Slater—and, really, all successful leaders—I began my own journey in becoming a leader without knowing very much about leadership.

For one thing, I lacked discipline. When I played high school basketball in my hometown of Milwaukee, I did all right, but I was no standout. Consequently, the big NCAA colleges didn't recruit me, and that's one reason I attended Stevens Point, a Division III NAIA school. As I look back on my time there, I'm glad I did—because of Dick Bennett, who went on to coach the University of Wisconsin Badgers and the Washington State University Cougars with great success. Coach Bennett taught me the virtues of discipline, and that was the thing I needed most when I stepped on campus. He demonstrated to me and to all of his players that you have to be diligent and work hard at your craft to get better every day. He showed us that you need to make a plan and work that plan. And you also have to use discipline to put your team first.

Although Dudley doesn't use the word *discipline* in this book, he certainly indicates that it's an important leadership trait. For example, he talks about the difficulty of putting the team first and the struggle he faced whenever his selfish ego, as he puts it, wanted one thing that would benefit him and the collective ego (which serves the needs of the organization) wanted something else. Placing the collective ego first in order to build a successful team takes discipline.

GETTING BUY-IN FROM THE STARS

Pat Riley and Gregg Popovich taught me a lot about team building. In different ways, they were able to fully integrate themselves within the team and build rapport and a solid winning system while still maintaining their leadership. Dudley and some of the other leaders who contributed to *Fusion Leadership* talk about working among the frontline employees and how critical it is to build a culture of mutual respect. Riley, Pop, and other coaches do this, and I also try to do it at the University of Portland with my players and with the other teams I've coached.

As a head coach—or CEO, department manager, college dean, director of a non-profit, law firm managing partner, or any other sort of leader—you are the salesperson for your philosophy and your culture and what you want to see that culture execute. Consequently, you have to get the top few people to buy into your vision and mission. You have to spend a lot of time with them, teaching them about the culture, because they have to be your voice in the locker room. I saw Riley do that with the two superstars on his Miami Heat team in the 1990s, Alonzo Mourning and Tim Hardaway. He was tough on them, demanded certain things from them, and held them accountable. (Pop's famous for this, too.)

Riley essentially put it this way: "I expressed to you the important points of how to build this culture, and I want you to come along with me." They did. They bought into Riley's vision and mission and helped sell it to the other players.

Dudley calls this *the ripple effect*, and I love that description. Your top senior performers, as well as your young up-and-comers, see your actions as the leader and how you handle a certain situation, and they enthusiastically sing the praises of the organization. This enthusiasm and their belief in the culture ripple out. And like my colleague Magic Johnson's smile, they become infectious.

One of the contributors to *Fusion Leadership*, Jeff Pinneo, was the president and CEO of Horizon Air. In chapter 3, he talks about one of his leadership tools: After every flight he was on landed, he'd let all the other passengers exit the plane first so he could help the flight attendants pick up any garbage left behind. That's something else—the CEO checking seatback pockets for trash! You can bet the flight crew loved it too and told others about it, putting the ripple effect into motion.

You see this in basketball, as well. When the last guy or gal on the bench—who also adds value to the team—sees the star players diving for a loose ball or making the extra pass to the open shooter, he or she will also put the selfish ego aside to serve the collective ego and move the team forward.

I tell my guys it's important that each of them have individual success but that it's more important that individual success leads to team success—which means everybody will be successful.

"So guys," I tell them, "make the extra pass, set the hard screen, and sacrifice your body to take a charge."

You can see this philosophy in all the great sports franchises, those that are run well and have a history of success: the San Antonio Spurs, the New England Patriots, the St. Louis Cardinals, and—I'd like to think—the Portland Trail Blazers team that I was a part of in the late 1980s and early 1990s. In these systems, you don't want to let your brother down. You've got each other's back. Everybody has a piece of ownership. You're going to do everything you can to make sure another player doesn't fail, and you know that your teammates are going to do everything they can to make sure you don't fail. When there's a breakdown, everyone's going to come together. That's the culture you see in the teams and the organizations that are successful.

In San Antonio, Pop would tell his players to leave their egos at the door. Rick Adelman sent the same message to the Trail Blazer players. The challenge, of course, is always with the alpha dogs. But the great teams I've been involved with, both as a player and as a coach, had very talented players who were always willing to work to make everybody better. They would ask, "How can I help you? How can I build you up so when we get to the playoffs, you have the confidence and the ability to use your tools and help us win?"

Dudley asked me if I thought more than one alpha dog can coexist on a sports team or in an organization, and, if so, if the principles in the book allow more alpha dogs to coexist on the same team and succeed.

This is what I told him: "With Fusion Leadership, you can have as many alpha dogs as you want, as long as they all deliver the same message and have the same agenda. The tools in the book will definitely allow the alpha dogs to coexist and come together, use these tools, and make sure everyone feels valued. And that's the beauty of it—finding that perfect synergy within a group of colleagues who all may have great talent but still keep the bigger picture in mind and work together to realize greater collective success. It's a leader's job to foster a culture that encourages this."

LISTEN AND LET OTHERS SHINE

Another principle that helps shape the Fusion Leadership model is the idea that a leader doesn't always have to show he or she is the smartest person in the room. Dudley tells a great story about how he learned this the hard way. I agree that, even if you're the most accomplished leader in your profession, you sometimes have to step back and let others shine. And the first thing you have to do is recognize that you're always going to have smart people around. You want to have people who are very knowledgeable in both your own areas of expertise and also in those in which you lack knowledge. You want different perspectives. You need to truly listen, and, when you do, you need to demonstrate that you have confidence in your colleagues.

When you constantly interrupt someone—as was the case in Dudley's story—you're essentially telling that person they're not doing it right. As a result, you're harming or maybe even destroying their self-confidence. When this happens, and they come into a situation where you need them to be confident and lead, they won't be able to, because you always cut in front of them. They're thinking, *Okay, when is he going to come and do that again?*

In basketball, this happens in a timeout fairly quickly. You're trying to solve the situation on the fly, and you're always getting cut off. But sometimes the coach should just sit back (perhaps not at the end of a close game when he or she should diagram a winning play) and ask the question: How are we going to fix this? I've been around a lot of coaches who say, "Okay guys, how are we going to fix this? You're out there; I'm not. You need to fix it." This empowers them.

I've touched on a few of the tools that *Fusion Leadership* offers. But, of course, there are more, as well as different and intriguing examples of the ones I mentioned. While this leadership model resonates with me and I recognize that I already use some of the techniques in my own coaching, I learned about many more tactics that I intend to place in my leadership arsenal and apply both on the court and off. I wish I could have read *Fusion Leadership* years ago, but I'm so glad I've read it now. It serves as both a validation of the principles I believe in and a guiding source of advice and inspiration for the future.

HOW DO YOU FOSTER ENTHUSIASM?

The statistics stagger the mind. Some 70 percent of the nation's workforce hates their jobs, according to several recent surveys. These workers simply find little to no value in what they do for a living and don't want to go to work on Monday morning—or, for that matter, any other morning. They don't fulfill a universal desire that we, as humans, share: the need to find meaning in our work. Many of these disgruntled workers serve bosses who, quite frankly, don't care whether their employees are satisfied and passionate about what they do on the job. These CEOs and vice presidents and managers and supervisors are leaders in name only and merely look out for their own interests, their own paycheck and perks, and their own prestige and power.

The leadership tools and techniques articulated in this book can fundamentally change that bleak reality.

Imagine, if you will, that those percentages were flipped, that, instead of the 70:30 ratio of dissatisfied workers, nearly three-quarters of American workers *were* satisfied and able to feed the churning, burning hunger we all have to find meaning in our work. If 70 percent of us felt real job satisfaction, that we were making our corner of society better, collectively, we'd change the world.

If that seems farfetched, think again, because, if you're reading this, you likely are (or aspire to be) a leader in your organization, on one level or another, and that means you're already in a position to enrich the lives of those in your charge, which, in turn, would improve your organization and your own life. Fortunately, many work groups, companies, and organizations have leaders who do understand that, by finding ways to feed their employees' hunger for meaning in their jobs, they're tapping into one of the most powerful forces on Planet Earth: the power of a committed workforce with a common passion.

We need more leaders who understand and act on this need for value and worth on the job. Otherwise, with the status quo as it is, we're failing to mine vast untapped resources—human intellect, spirit, creativity, and productivity. If we could activate that dormant human potential and inspire our companies, departments, teams, and work groups with vision, purpose, and passion, we could generate new life-saving drugs and life-enhancing products and services, cultivate innovative agricultural crops, invent more clean-energy technologies, and tackle such crises as climate change and global poverty and famine.

When leaders unleash this force, when they give their employees opportunities to discover and nurture on-the-job enthusiasm and gratification, they get so much in return. Their actions set in motion a symbiotic cycle. When you see those you're leading quench that thirst for meaning in their work and find fulfillment, you too experience self-fulfillment—not to mention increased revenues, higher profits, better perks and per diems, and other material gains—because you know that you helped create that happy workforce.

FUSING OUR COLLECTIVE ENERGY

As cofounder and chief executive officer of Integra Telecom (which briefly changed its name to Electric Lightwave and then announced its purchase by the Zayo Group [NYSE: Zayo] in 2016), I experienced the magic that's created when a workforce of several thousand people commit to a common cause. But the magic didn't just manifest—well—magically. It was hard work. I reaped the rewards—both those that fill the bank account and those that feed the soul—by making strategic moves, with my management team, in an approach I've come to call *Fusion Leadership*.

This book offers readers a toolbox of real-life, tried-and-tested techniques that comprise the Fusion Leadership philosophy and practice through workplace stories from me, a prestigious group of CEOs, other managers, and executives who adhere to a similar leadership style and generously contributed their input to this narrative. Many of these luminaries have embraced *servant leadership*, a concept that has been around for a very long time but that was coined, famously, by Robert Greenleaf in a 1970 essay entitled "The Servant as Leader." In it, Greenleaf wrote this:

> The servant-leader *is* servant first . . . It begins with the natural feeling that one wants to serve, to serve *first*. Then conscious choice brings one to aspire to lead. That person is sharply different from one who is *leader* first, perhaps because of the need to assuage an unusual power drive or to acquire material possessions. . . . The leader-first and the servant-first are two extreme types.

While I think of myself as a servant leader, I struggle with the notion of magnanimous service as I understand that to be a core tenet of servant leadership. For example, in his essay "The Case for Servant Leadership," originally published by the Greenleaf Center for Servant Leadership in 2008, Kent McKeith states that servant leaders "don't worry about their own personal status or prestige."

Let's be real. I don't believe we humans are wired that way. While I aspire to the ideal of placing others first, the highest-functioning people I know, on their best days, place the welfare of others as an equal priority to their own selfish interests. The highly competitive, career-challenging demands of Western capitalism draw on the self-serving survival instincts programmed into our psyches by our ancestors. And that's fine, as long as our actions also serve to advance the interests of our colleagues and our society.

Here lies the key point: When our selfish actions cross the line of diminishing the effectiveness of our team, we commit the ultimate failure in leadership.

Fusion Leadership acknowledges the inherent and genuine struggle between rewarding our selfish ego and rewarding our organization, or the collective ego. What's more, it also recognizes that, in this selfish-ego-versus-collective-ego struggle, the act of prioritizing the needs of the organization is not a selfless act. It is ultimately very self-serving, which is okay. In fact, some people subscribe to the theory that all human behavior is self-serving, which is a philosophic precept for another time and another book, although I touch on it in these pages.

So Fusion Leadership is not philanthropic. It's about creating world-class results for your organization through helping others find meaning in their jobs. It's also about fusing teams of people together to achieve those results. Now, it's important to know that I didn't lead my company based on some sort of managerial blueprint to forge the success we achieved. Rather, I cobbled it together bit by bit along the way, sometimes stumbling and bumbling and sometimes making decisions based in part on raw emotions—like fear.

DEALING WITH THE INTIMIDATING TONY

When I became the leader of Integra Telecom, I was terrified. I didn't start the company from scratch but, rather, through the acquisition of a modest-sized business with less than $1 million in revenue and a small but tight-knit workforce. As cofounder and newly minted chief executive officer, I was clearly in charge of the company, but I was intimidated by the workers—all nine of them.

I had very little experience managing people, but there I was, responsible for leading the technicians and call-center people. And I was the ultimate outsider. Because of my education at prestigious schools and my subsequent career moves, I had always been surrounded by highly educated people who performed intellectual-type work. All of a sudden, I was responsible for managing people who hadn't gone to the top universities—or perhaps hadn't gone to college at all. These frontline employees were hard-working, smart people but, in part because of my own insecurities about not knowing how to relate to them or what they might think of me or how they might react to me being the boss, I was frightened.

I was especially afraid of a man I'll call Tony.

Tony intimidated me because he was from New Jersey and had the classic tough East Coast attitude. He was an engineer and a no-nonsense, in-your-face guy. I don't know if he had an engineering degree, but it was obvious to me that he was incredibly smart. He served as the company's engineer and had garnered the respect of the entire organization—that is, the other eight people. If you said something that was wrong or uninformed or if you offered an idea that would move the organization in a direction that Tony was uncomfortable with, it was like a load of bricks coming down on you, and the other eight people would quickly know about it. In short, if you got on the wrong side of Tony, your credibility was shot. So I was extremely sensitive about how I would interact with him. He was my litmus test, in a way. If I could win Tony over, I thought, I could manage almost anybody.

But I knew it wouldn't be easy. We were very different people. I was from the West Coast and lived in the upscale West Hills neighborhood of Portland, Oregon. Tony lived in a middle-class suburb of Portland. I had formal technical training, earned an MBA at Harvard, and, as an introvert, I was anything but intimidating.

Tony would crack jokes about Harvard MBAs. Here's one: *How many Harvard MBAs does it take to screw in a light bulb? . . . Just one. He grasps it firmly, and the universe revolves around him.* Tony was sarcastic about people who are "too smart for their own good." He'd say, when I was in earshot, "What good are they when it comes to the realities of making a telecom network work and taking care of customers? The last thing we need around here is a Harvard MBA."

In our early interactions, I remember visiting Tony in his office, which was the switching room where we kept our network gear. He'd be surrounded by all these blinking lights and computer terminals that were controlling the network. He wore reading glasses and would literally look down his nose at me, over the top his glasses, as I walked into his domain to ask him a question. He always made me feel like I was needlessly interrupting him. He was kind of like the master heart surgeon in the middle of surgery, and you'd better be careful how you behave around this maestro, because it could really have a dramatic impact on the health of the patient. Have I mentioned that he was intimidating?

At times, I felt like matching his demeanor and asserting my authority; I was, after all, the boss. If I chose to, I could roll up my sleeves, flex my muscles, puff out my chest, and issue an it's-my-way-or-the-highway edict. But, even though I had technical training, I didn't know anything about this complex switching network and the different devices that connected fiber cables together, which allowed our small number of customers to maintain their communication. The last thing I wanted to do was drive away Tony—the one guy who made it all work.

So I assumed a walking-on-eggshells approach with him, manufacturing rapport slowly. I hoped our relationship would evolve organically and that we'd develop a partnership built on mutual respect. I took many deep breaths and expended a lot of patience in my interactions with him, but, honestly, I didn't undertake this investment in Tony because I knew anything about effective leadership or had any appreciation for where the company might go. I certainly couldn't have predicted how much Integra Telecom would grow or that this kind of delicate handling of a challenging but vital employee would become an important tenet in my leadership philosophy, one of the many tools that smart leaders use to move their organizations forward. I just wanted our network to function properly. I wanted Tony to be a contributing member of the team. That was my focus. And on top of that, as I said, I was simply frightened.

WINNING TONY OVER:
FROM SKEPTIC TO EVANGELIST

But, as you've probably guessed by now, that fear dissipated, and I ended up earning Tony's confidence and respect. All the baby steps I'd been taking to fabricate a relationship with him were beginning to work, and then I made a pivotal move that won him over. In the wake of the Telecommunications Act of 1996, a new breed of telecom companies emerged, and Integra Telecom was the first in Oregon to purchase and install a switching network that was comparable to those used by such telecom heavyweights as Verizon and AT&T. It was Tony's job to install this complex equipment and get it working.

One of my roles was to negotiate the installation contract with the vendor Lucent, which came out of Bell Labs and had supplied much of the switching networks for AT&T and the Bell companies. This was a huge, multinational, multibillion-dollar technology company that had built the telecom infrastructure for our country, and I was stepping between the ropes and into the ring to negotiate the contract. Lucent gave us the form of agreement that they doled out to everybody, but it contained a few things that weren't right for us. I ended up becoming a pain in the ass to Lucent—even introverts can get under the skin—because I made a point of stopping the negotiations and forcing them to deal with a couple of issues that were important to us out in the industrial park in Hillsboro, Oregon, where Integra Telecom was located.

These issues were a little bit unusual. Not only were they important to me from a contractual standpoint; they were important to the network. And the network was all-important to Tony. He saw that I deftly negotiated and stubbornly fought for and won the contract changes. Although I'd been working day by day to build rapport with Tony by investing energy in our interactions and going out of my way to get his opinions on business operations, that contract victory served as the tipping point in our relationship.

Soon after those negotiations, Tony invited me and one or two other people from the company to come over and have dinner at his house. His parents were coming to town from New Jersey, and he wanted me to meet them. I really hit it off with his parents, and from that point forward, things went well with Tony and me; we became close colleagues and friends. Building a relationship of mutual respect is what made it happen.

While I knew that I needed Tony, his knowledge base, and his influence over the other employees, I had no idea just how important he'd become as Integra Telecom grew. I didn't know the significance of what was incubating as I forged a strong bond between us. He went on to become one of our long-time engineering leaders and accomplished great things for the organization. He stayed with us for many years, building and rebuilding the network until we ultimately operated in eleven states. And, importantly, he became a great evangelist for Integra Telecom, singing our praises to those both inside and outside the company.

As I've recounted, during my first several months as Integra Telecom's CEO, I felt a lot of discomfort as I groped for my own leadership identity. But, somehow, I started to stumble onto some of the practices that later became second nature to me and helped me move the company forward.

As Integra Telecom expanded geographically, we also grew and prospered, becoming one of the ten largest fiber-based, land-line telecommunications companies in the United States. We transformed Integra Telecom from a start-up firm into one with twenty-five hundred workers and a market value of nearly $2 billion. With our leadership and our committed and impassioned employees, we built one of the fastest-growing and most profitable companies in our industry. Wall Street analysts commonly made the point that we were literally twice as profitable as our industry-peer-group average.

By any measure, that's a strong record of accomplishment. When I left my CEO role at Integra Telecom, I spent much of the next year asking myself this question: Why was Integra Telecom so successful? When I became CEO, I didn't set out to assemble one of the ten largest telecom companies in our industry sector, able to compete with Verizon and AT&T. I was really just looking for the entrepreneurial benefits of not having a boss and being in charge of myself. That's what I was focused on. And yet this company became wildly successful.

HOW DID I GET HERE?
A JOURNEY OF EXPLORATION

So I embarked on a journey, spending a year pondering how in the world it all happened. I'm reminded of the Talking Heads song "Once in a Lifetime," in which the incomparable David Byrne belts out existential musings, questioning how he got to where he is. (I'm paraphrasing, but if you know the song, you're probably singing the lyrics in your head. If you don't, look them up sometime; they're intelligently compelling and witty as well.)

The more I thought about this question—*How did I get here?*—the more intrigued I became about the reasons for the success of Integra Telecom and the decisions I made, both the good ones and the bad ones, as its leader. The telecom industry is the last place I would recommend to anybody to go start a business. The barriers to entry are enormous; it requires billions of dollars in capital. I was arguably half crazy to even start the company—yet we had all that success. I ended up concluding that the key to our prosperity was what I mentioned early in this introduction: the amazing power of several thousand people who shared a common passion and commitment to build the company. I became fascinated by the ways that my team and I, like many other leaders, helped ignite and harness that power. How do you create this passion and commitment? Why do some companies succeed and others fail?

Of course, many organizations are led by people who latch onto the top-down leadership model. The CEOs who embrace and practice within this power model are highly dynamic figures, seemingly bigger than life. When they walk into the room, they remove the oxygen because all the attention is focused on them. And they love it. They live for it. They approach leadership from the perspective that it's their own sheer magnetism and their raw capacity to be brilliant and demanding that makes the company successful. Hollywood loves these power-model-loving CEOs—think of the character

Michael Douglas played in the movie *Wall Street*—because they're very charismatic, confident, and captivating, even if they do believe, consciously or subconsciously, that "the collective ego be damned!"

While a lot of successful companies are managed by leaders like that, they run the risk of leaving their frontline employees behind and trampling over those people, not necessarily intentionally, but in a way that fails to build a work environment in which people respect one another. That's the real difference between the Fusion Leadership model and the power model.

I know plenty of these dictator-type CEOs, but, fortunately, I also know a lot of CEOs and other leaders who place the needs of frontline employees at the top of their priority list, and not simply for altruistic reasons. They do it because that's what gets results for the entire organization, and they understand that when the organization wins, they win. In essence, they know how to walk the tightrope across the selfish-ego-versus-collective-ego chasm.

So, beginning in 2011, the year I left Integra Telecom, I decided to take my journey of exploration—my quest to see how we create a shared passion in an organization—on the road and talk to other CEOs who had done something special by unleashing the energy of a passionate workforce. These are people who founded or grew businesses with more than a billion dollars in market value; served more than a million people in the business; or somehow, in a measurable way, truly transformed their industry or profession. I learned a lot from these leaders and also had several of my fundamental tenets of Fusion Leadership affirmed.

One important thing I came to understand is that this magic that you can create as a leader transcends different industries and both for-profit and nonprofit arenas. It transcends the public sector as well as the government sector. Ray Davis figured it out in the banking world. Colleen Abdoulah figured it out in the cable television world, as did Dave Shaffer in the nonprofit world and General Robert Van Antwerp in the governmental world. These leaders and others were also kind enough to contribute the time to tell me their stories, which serve as examples of applying Fusion Leadership principles to real-world, workplace situations.

Demonstrating candor and exhibiting vulnerability, these leaders explore how they navigated the internal dilemma of serving their organizations' collective egos while balancing the needs of their selfish egos. Yes, they also mastered the "Succeeding in Business 101" components with a well-differentiated market strategy, strong distribution channels, lean and efficient operations, and the other requirements that fill the pages of many business books. I also discovered, importantly, that many of them share my mission and seek to start a national dialogue that encourages others to think critically about how they balance the two often-competing egos. That is the focus of this book.

When you read the chapters about these leaders, you'll see that many of the tools they used are very simple but produce profound results. They demonstrate that when you employ these techniques, you can transform any organization.

The stories and personal struggles shared by these CEOs entertained and also humbled me. The selfish ego seduces, making it hard to be a Fusion Leader. Chip Bergh's messaging of his vision for Procter & Gamble in Singapore contrasts with my own selfish-ego challenges in answering this question: *Who gets the spacious corner office with a view?* Chip's approach to this question left me wondering if Integra Telecom could have been even more successful had I declined the temptation of the corner office as he did when leading Procter & Gamble's Asian expansion.

I gained another insight from my discussions with these leaders: They don't all agree with everything I do. For example, I believed that true Fusion Leaders don't compensate themselves at significantly greater amounts than their fellow leaders, those just below them on the hierarchical ladder. The amount you pay yourself as a leader can be a little bit more but not grossly more than your next-level commanders. That was the philosophy I brought to Integra Telecom. I paid myself 10 or 15 percent more than the next-highest-paid person, which was a system that differed significantly from traditional corporate compensation practices. By doing that, I thought I was communicating this message: "I'm in the trenches with the rest of you. I'm not setting myself up to be better and certainly not grossly wealthier than you are." I felt I'd boosted the probability of creating trust and loyalty and grooming committed leaders who would partner with me and that, consequently, my success would be greater.

Well, I kind of expected to hear that same approach to compensation from these other enlightened CEOs. And, indeed, I did from most of them. But public records show that at least one of them earns three times as much as the next leader in the company. Yet this person's got a remarkable record of success with very loyal and committed people. The lesson I learned from discovering this is that there's not a prescribed one-size-fits-all formula here.

But mostly, I found a lot in common with the leaders I talked to, and chief among our shared beliefs about leadership is this guiding tenet: True leadership shows people how to connect and commit to a common cause and helps them understand how they're part of something bigger than themselves. In this tangible way, the Fusion Leader can put meals on the table and begin to satisfy that hunger we all experience, to find meaning in our work. This book explores principles and practices to do just that and, as a result, improve the lives of everyone in the organization—including those who lead.

I hope this book also helps advance the movement to transform the workplace, improve people's lives, and change the world.

CHAPTER 1

WHO DO YOU PRIORITIZE WITHIN YOUR ORGANIZATION?

WOW! WHAT A CONCERT: FRONT LINE TAKES CENTER STAGE AS LEADERSHIP ORCHESTRATES FIRM'S SUCCESS

At the start of a hot, muggy day in the summer of 2007, the general manager of the Cleveland, Ohio, office of WOW! gathered his team of technicians to meet with the CEO of the national cable and data firm, Colleen Abdoulah, who was visiting from WOW!'s Denver headquarters. Abdoulah was about to find out which technician she would accompany and work with in the field for a full day of installing cable lines. The GM pulled a name out of a makeshift hat and announced, "And the winner is . . . Terry!"

Terry, a technician who'd been slouched over in his seat, tilted his head back, stared at the ceiling, and, scowling, let this indiscretion slip from his lips: "Oh shit."

Everyone in the room laughed nervously, and several technicians stole glances at Abdoulah to see how their boss would react to Terry's verbal misstep. But the unflappable CEO quickly defused the situation. "Don't worry about it, Terry," she recalled saying. "We'll have a nice day today."

Well, "nice" would not be the best way to describe how that particular work day actually transpired, a day that tested Abdoulah's resolve to keep her selfish ego in check so as to advance the company's collective ego. But I'll get to that soon enough.

Gaining Customers, Winning Awards, and Building Value

When I met Colleen Abdoulah, I was struck by her intelligence, wit, optimism, and effervescent personality. As I got to know her better, I discovered that she has a dynamic yet humble leadership style, with an uncanny ability to motivate others. She's also a savvy businesswoman who knows how to achieve big-time results, leading WOW! to experience a string of successes that helped catapult the company to become one of the ten largest cable and data players in the United States.

When Abdoulah took the helm of WOW! in 2002, the company had $200 million in annual revenue and employed six hundred people in five markets. As of this writing, in the fall of 2016, WOW! generates $1.2 billion, has thousands of employees, and serves customers in nine states. That's impressive growth by almost anyone's standards. The firm has won a slew of awards, including seventeen first-place rankings in the prestigious J. D. Power and Associates consumer studies of telecom companies.

"A couple of years, we won the J. D. Power award in all three categories—cable, phone, and Internet," said Abdoulah, who's now retired from the company. "We've won the award over such [heavyweights] as Verizon, AT&T, Comcast, Time-Warner, Dish, and DirecTV. In the telecom industry, no other company has received that level of recognition from its customers. We have eight years of first-place recognition in *Consumer Reports* and have won the Readers' Choice Award of *PC Magazine* as the best Internet provider. And, in every market we've operated in, we've been chosen as the best employer to work with."

One reason WOW! succeeded in the market and received these accolades, including its best-employer status, is because Abdoulah and her team operated within what they call an internal "service structure," which places the company's frontline workers—well—front and center. The employees in the call centers and the technicians in the field serve as the firm's focal point, because they relate directly with the customer.

Abdoulah used a concert metaphor to describe WOW!'s customer-centered configuration. "The service structure puts the frontline workers on center stage as the top concert performers," she explained to me. "They're who the audience comes to see. And all the rest of us, from the CEO to the vice presidents, to the engineering department, to marketing, to legal—we were all there in the background, helping put the concert on, helping our front line perform. So by structuring it that way, you take away the hierarchy, the bureaucracy, the power-based model that so many corporations exist on, and you put the power and emphasis on the front line, the people dealing with the customers. They're the ones the customers talked to all the time, not me."

This model, in part, influenced the behavior of WOW!'s workforce: They were motivated to serve the customer the best they could. It also helped keep spirits up, both internally and externally. Not long ago, the company conducted a survey to determine its employees' and customers' happiness quotients. Both turned out to be very high. "We were at 97.3 percent internally," Abdoulah said. "With our customers, we were at 94.3 percent. And we believed there's a direct correlation between how happy employees feel and the happiness of the customers."

The service structure also ensured that members of management stay in touch with both the concert performers, to continue the analogy, and the audience. "We never wanted to make the mistake that too many companies make and that is allowing people in leadership to get too far away from the front line or too far away from the end customer," Abdoulah said, noting that focus groups and surveys help keep leaders in touch.

But another method seems to be particularly enlightening. "We had a program where all people who didn't have direct-line exposure or exposure to the end customer must go out once a quarter and listen, monitor phone calls. If you can get to one of our call centers, that's ideal. If not, you do it remotely. Then the next quarter, you'd go out with a technician and work for a day in the field. If your schedule was really tight, you'd do half a day. But we preferred that you do the full day."

On-the-Job Odd Couple

And that, of course, gets us back to that summer day in the field in Cleveland. A half an hour after she learned that Terry would be her colleague for the day, Abdoulah—dressed in jeans, a WOW! t-shirt, and boots—walked with the apologetic general manager to the parking lot lined with service trucks. "I'm so sorry about Terry's reaction," the GM told his CEO, referring to the technician's obscenity. "He's only been with us for about eight months."

"That's fine. No problem," Abdoulah said, as they approached Terry, who was frantically cleaning up his truck. As the two unlikely field partners got into the vehicle, Abdoulah gave Terry her usual spiel, what she said to all the technicians she accompanied on the job: "I told him, 'I don't want you to treat me like a dumb girl. I'm here to help. Don't treat me like the CEO. I'm to be your assistant. I want to learn from you. I want to observe what you go through during your day. So put me to work.'"

Now, when most WOW! technicians heard Abdoulah say this, they simply said, "Okay, Colleen," and then, when they arrived at a customer's house, they handed her an information packet, introduced her to the customer, and had her sit and converse with the customer as the technician performed the installation.

"Not this guy," Abdoulah told me. "Terry said, 'Oh really?' and threw a map at me, saying, 'We're on a new route today. I don't know where we're going, so you find the address off the work order and tell me where to go.'"

The problem was—she didn't know how to read a map. "So I said, 'Okay, Terry, I guess I am kind of a dumb girl. I don't know how to read a map.' He quickly showed me how, handed me a phone and gave me orders. He said, 'So you know our policy. Call the customer and tell them we're on our way.'"

Clearly, the corporate boss was not the one in charge on this trip. But she knew exactly what she was doing.

When they arrived at the customer's three-story, brick colonial home, they discovered that the representative at the call center had made a mistake. She had put in the work order as a reconnect, which doesn't require much time. But, in fact, it was a new installation; the moving van was even there. "So we knew this was going to be a much longer job, and we'd have to redo our whole day," Abdoulah said. "Terry handed me the phone— and he was a little angry—and said, 'You're going to have to call dispatch and reroute the rest of my jobs. We're going to be here a good three or four hours.'"

Well, Abdoulah had never called dispatch. She was clueless but figured it out. And then she asked the customers—a husband and wife—if they wanted upgrades and additional services. They did, which is good for business, but it also meant the installation became more complicated. "So Terry and I were going back out to the truck, and he said, 'We're going to have to go onto the pole. Get the ladder and meet me out back.'"

A little later, Terry called from the yard: "What's taking you so long?" Abdoulah was struggling with the ladder, unable to get it off the truck, frustrated, and feeling more incompetent by the minute. Terry saw this and told Abdoulah, "Well, you've got the safety latch on. You know how to take the safety latch off, right?"

At that point, Abdoulah turned to the technician and said, "Look, I *am* the CEO. I have not taken ladder training. Can you just take it down and show me?" He did, and instead of hauling the ladder himself, he showed her how to carry it safely and walked away.

"So I followed this guy carrying this heavy-ass ladder," Abdoulah recalled with a laugh, "and, needless to say, during the next few hours, he had me climbing the pole, helping him ground the cable, wiring the house, drilling in the closet, up in the attic. I mean, I worked so hard that day and learned so much about what we do and how we do it."

"That Explains It"

Abdoulah also learned what these customers thought of WOW! and their impression of her on-the-job efforts. At one point during her "apprentice" day, she was in the master suite, cleaning up the shavings from drilling, and the wife was making the bed. They had this exchange:

"I love your company," the woman told Abdoulah.

"Thank you. So do I," Abdoulah replied.

"I really shopped around a lot, and you're not by any means the cheapest, but your phone people are so nice, and now I see that your technician is too. Everybody I've come into contact with from your company is so knowledgeable and nice, and they make us feel really special."

"I love to hear that. That's great."

"Can I ask you how long you've been doing this?" the woman asked.

"Well, to be honest, I don't really do this. I'm the CEO of the company, and I'm out to help our employee and learn what goes on in the field."

"Oh my god, that explains it. Honey, come here," the woman said, beckoning her husband.

Her husband came into the bedroom and she said, "Honey, she's the CEO. She's not a technician."

"Oh, that explains it," the man said.

"Explains what?" Abdoulah wanted to know.

So the woman did explain: "We've been commenting all day while you've been here that this is such a great company. Everybody is so knowledgeable at what they do—that is, except you."

"Well," Abdoulah told me, chuckling, "we all had a good laugh. But I'll tell you we have a WOW! A Friend referral program, and we must have gotten three or four referrals from that woman."

Abdoulah ate her lunch in the truck en route to the next install job, worked all afternoon and into the early evening, and came home exhausted. "I've always had an appreciation for what our call-center reps go through—they take up to ten thousand calls a year," she said. "And I've also had a great appreciation for what our field people do—in the winter or summer in the rain, snow, heat, and humidity. But when you actually do the work they do, you go from an appreciation of them intellectually to an appreciation of what they do physically."

After hearing this story, I asked a couple of questions: "Colleen, as you know, I've also worked alongside the frontline people at an Integra Telecom call center, and it's not easy. What you do—working in the field—is much more difficult, especially on that particular day. Terry ordered you around, worked you pretty hard, and didn't pull any punches. Did you ever feel like saying *Forget this. I'm the CEO and I don't have to do this!*? Did you ever feel like saying *To hell with the collective ego and the common good of working with the technician and learning about his job!*? Did you want to pull rank?"

As I expected, she was very honest with me: "I didn't like that Terry got short with me and was impatient because I didn't know how to drill properly, didn't know how to ground the cable. Internally, my temper flared. My selfish ego was like, 'Are you serious, buddy? You're talking to me with that tone of voice? You're ordering me around?!' But I had to reflect to myself and say, 'He's the expert here, and he's trying to get this done right and in a time frame that allows us to get the rest of our work done. I just have to appreciate that and do what he's telling me. I'm here to learn and to stay connected with the frontline employees and the customers. It's all worth it.'"

WOW! Moments: Good for the Soul, Good for Business

When Abdoulah became the CEO, she and her team changed the name of the company from Wide Open West to WOW! and embarked on a rebranding effort that supported a culture in which employees nurture relationships with each other and their customers. "Our philosophical statement was to deliver an employee and customer experience that lived up to our name," she said.

The new culture manifested in many ways, including a new

twist on titles. Yes, Abdoulah had been the CEO (and chairwoman of the board), but on the company website that moniker came second, below descriptors of who she was as a person: "Mother, Hugger, Keeper of the Culture." The chief financial officer had this primary description of who he is: "Family Man, Dog Lover, Teammate." The senior vice president for human resources was described as: "Mom, Book Lover, Jazz Enthusiast."

This wasn't just a feel-good gimmick; it got to the heart of Abdoulah's leadership approach and WOW!'s strategically conceived work environment. It seemed to resonate well with customers, too. "When people engaged with us, we wanted them to engage with us as a person, not as a technician or call-center rep or IT guy or CEO, but as a person who is a golfer, a reader, a foodie—whatever their descriptors are," Abdoulah explained. "I remember when we messed up on something with a customer and that person wrote one of our marketing people and really blasted him and then said, 'PS: I see you're a vegetarian. So am I, and I've got some great vegetarian recipes.' And—boom—they connected on the recipe side of things, and the service thing—which we resolved quickly—became secondary to their bond as two vegetarians. That's the way we should be navigating through our daily lives—not based on our titles or positions but on who we are as people."

Another embodiment of the company's culture—and a way it differentiated itself in the marketplace—is through what are called *WOW! Moments*, which are written and talked about and often publicly acknowledged within the company's community. The firm website describes a WOW! Moment as "an unexpected act of courtesy and kindness." The explanation continues: "Sometimes the moment can represent a large gesture, but more often than not, it's the little things that can make you smile or brighten your day. At WOW! we strive to create these WOW! Moments for anyone we might encounter in the communities we serve. It's part of our company culture. And we do it not just because it's good business but because we are committed to doing our part to make a positive difference in the lives that we touch."

Now, I'm sure that WOW! employees, starting with Abdoulah,

do strive to make "a positive difference." But make no mistake: WOW! Moments were and are, indeed, good for business.

Here Kitty, Kitty

Consider this story that unfolded in early 2009 with a customer named Karen in the Detroit area. Abdoulah received a three-page letter from Karen that praised WOW! and explained how her family and friends had told her to become a WOW! customer, which she had done two weeks earlier. But then she said that ever since the technician had come to her house to do the installation, her cat of ten years had been missing. Karen attached a lost-pet poster to her letter, complete with a picture of her cat, with which she had blanketed her neighborhood—but to no avail. A couple of her neighbors told Karen that they suspected the cable installer of stealing her cat.

"She wrote," Abdoulah recalled, "that the technician 'was very friendly with my cat, petting her and saying that he loved cats and was thinking of getting one. So I want to know if your guy took my cat. Would you please investigate?'"

Abdoulah knew the technician and also knew that he'd never do such a thing. She chuckled and thought about throwing the letter in the garbage. Then she stopped and thought, *Wait a minute. This could turn into a WOW! Moment.* And with that, Abdoulah asked a couple of employees to go to the technician's house to see if he had Karen's cat. He didn't, of course, but he did feel very bad that the feline had gone missing and blamed himself, thinking the cat had gotten out the door when he was coming and going during the installation.

So Abdoulah phoned Karen—who initially didn't believe WOW!'s CEO was calling her—and told her that she sent people to investigate the technician's home and he did not have her cat. Karen thanked Abdoulah for taking her seriously and looking into the situation, because the kitty meant so much to her, and she said she hoped she hadn't gotten the technician in trouble because "he's such a nice young man."

Then Abdoulah walked the proverbial extra mile. "I told Karen that he's not in trouble and that I've had cats and dogs and I love both," she recalled. "I said, 'If it would help to get over this loss, we would like to buy you a cat. What kind would you like?' Well, Karen started crying and said, 'You would do that for me?'" But she declined the offer, saying she had just gotten laid off from her job, already had a dog and another cat at home, and couldn't really afford the expense of veterinarian bills and food for a new pet.

Two weeks passed, and Abdoulah received a phone call from Karen, who said, "Colleen, it's me, Karen, the cat lady. I want you to know that my cat came home. He's thinner, and he has frostbite in his paws, but he's home."

Abdoulah expressed her happiness and then listened while Karen explained that, a week or so previously, the technician bought Karen a month's worth of cat and dog food and hand-delivered the pet gift basket. "He told me that he was sorry that the cat had gotten out and that hopefully the food would help with my other cat and dog for the next month or so," Karen said, through tears. "Anyway, thank you for caring, Colleen."

End of story—almost.

Good Deed, Good Business Practice

About that good-for-business part . . . Abdoulah's leadership in this WOW! Moment, or series of moments—the technician's concern and subsequent pet food delivery and, in a larger sense, the corporate culture in which WOW! operates—all translated into revenue generation. That is, Karen's daughter and a few of her neighbors left the competition to come to WOW!

This anecdote illustrates a couple of themes that constitute the Fusion Leadership model. First, let's look back at the moment when my friend read Karen's letter, chuckled, and pondered throwing it—and all the sentiment behind it—into the garbage. She paused and had to consider her choice, probably quickly or even subconsciously. She surely wasn't eager to make the call to investigate the technician, which might make her look untrusting of him, overly sentimental about Karen and her wayward cat, or even downright foolish, while putting the "investigators" in an awkward spot and potentially alienating the technician. In other words, there was some risk involved.

This is a classic case of the selfish ego versus the collective ego. Fortunately, Abdoulah set her self-centered mindset aside, looked long-term, and made the collective-ego choice.

She ruminated about that decision with me. "What captured me was Karen's first paragraph of her letter," she said. "We put a lot of emphasis on our WOW! A Friend referral program. At least 40 percent of our connects came from word of mouth. We didn't have enough coverage in the metro areas we served to justify advertising in traditional media like radio, TV, and newspaper, so much of our marketing and sales were door-to-door, direct mail, and a lot of emphasis on word of mouth. Our reputation was critical. So when Karen essentially said, 'I finally switched from the competition to WOW! because my family members and friends who were WOW! customers were telling me what a great experience they've had, and then I lose my cat,' I couldn't ignore her."

Another way this story reflects Fusion Leadership is through the manifestation of the ripple effect. When I asked Abdoulah about this, she didn't hesitate to answer: "For a leader to have an impact, to serve others in a powerful and influential way, those others who they're serving need to know what the leader is passionate about. I think the people in our organization knew that I and the other leaders of WOW! were incredibly passionate about our customers and our employees. So when I did what I did with Karen, they didn't roll their eyes and say, 'Is she crazy?' They thought, 'Wow, she cares about that lady. I need to care, too.'"

I'm guessing that the installer who bought the pet food felt the ripple effect. After all, he knew that his CEO took time out of her day to read Karen's letter and make the difficult call to have his house checked out, looking for the lost cat. Abdoulah said she thinks his action was motivated more by the work environment that WOW! had in place. "Our culture encouraged us to create WOW! Moments for each other, family members, customers," she explained. "When you feel something, it's okay to act, and the installer felt very deep remorse about the cat getting out, and he wanted to act on that. It was his natural instinct, and the culture we created supported his decision to help Karen. We celebrated feeling and behavior like that. We expected it."

Hearing from Customers, Sharing with Employees

Abdoulah loved hearing how members of her workforce treated customers with dignity, patience, and respect. A few years ago, for example, she received an email from a woman whose husband of forty-eight years had recently died. Naturally, the widow had been in a very dark place, grieving her spouse's death. Finally, after several months, she got around to dealing with the technology in the house, which he had always taken care of.

"She wrote to me," Abdoulah recalled, "that she had to talk to our call center three different times, and, as she said, 'All three times, I got a different representative, and all three times, they must have spent fifteen to twenty minutes with me, and they were kind, patient, knowledgeable, and understanding. The third person had to send a technician to my home because I wasn't getting what the representative was explaining to me. He came, and not only was he on time, but he wore his booties in my house and was kind and knowledgeable. When I told him my story, he even helped me with a few things around my house.'"

But it was the last line of her letter that got to Abdoulah. The woman wrote, "Whoever thought calling my cable company would help me get over my grief." And that statement has stayed with the CEO—or rather, the Mother, Hugger, Keeper of the Culture. "I still get emotional telling the story," she said.

Then there was a father who wrote to Abdoulah in late 2008 after the economic meltdown. He had just suffered through a horrible divorce and had gained custody of his three kids. He had to take a different job that paid more but required him to travel. He was on a business trip when his oldest child called in a panic. "We had temporarily disconnected their services for nonpayment," Abdoulah recalled.

Here's what the man told her: "I was panicked because I didn't mean not to pay. I was just so overwhelmed that I'd forgotten. So I called the collection department at WOW! and started to tell my story. Your representative cut me off halfway through. I thought he was going to tell me, 'Sorry buddy, we're not going to turn on your services until you pay.' But instead, he said, 'Sir, you can stop now. I've heard enough. You've been through a lot. I've turned your services back on, and when you get back into town, you can pay us when you can. I know you will.' He also said he could put me on auto-pay so I would never make that mistake again, which was a good idea. I want you to know that I will never switch to another provider, because through this whole trauma, I was treated with such respect and kindness and understanding."

Abdoulah shared both of these WOW! Moments with her workforce, which enriched the culture even further and motivated employees to provide top-notch customer service. And, from a business standpoint, the sharing of these experiences helped maintain WOW!'s high retention rate at all levels. "Our average call-center tenure was seven years, and if you know anything about call centers, you know that's amazing," Abdoulah said. "Everybody understood that WOW! Moments helped create experiences and built loyalty and retention, which lead to growth. As long as we were holding onto customers and gaining new customers and operating efficiently, we had a sustained business model and continued to compete and succeed in a highly competitive environment."

Getting Tough, Sending Messages

But, as we all know, no matter what career you're in, life on the job isn't always warm and fuzzy. Some people can be . . . well, to be tame, let's just say they can be less than pleasant.

As mentioned above, in addition to accompanying technicians into the field, Abdoulah also listened in on calls from time to time. Once, she heard an exchange between one of WOW!'s call representatives and an abusive customer. "Our rep was doing everything she could to defuse this guy," Abdoulah said, adding that she knew she had to intervene. "I introduced myself, and I asked the rep to hang up. I said to the customer that 'if anyone in our organization ever spoke to a customer the way you were speaking to our employee, we would terminate that person.' And I said, 'As of this hour, I'm terminating you as a customer. There will be two service technicians at your home to disconnect your service.' Well, he swore me up one side and down the other and yelled, 'You can't do that!' I said, 'Yes I can, and if you resist, we'll have the police there.'"

That really set the man off, calling Abdoulah every name in the book, punctuating his obscenity-laced onslaught with one f-bomb after another, and threatening to go to WOW!'s competition, to which Abdoulah calmly said, "That's fine, sir. It will be their loss and our gain."

My friend understood and put in practice a fundamental tenet of responsible leadership: If you're going to hold your own people to a certain high-level standard, you must have their backs and protect them when need be. That's one way to build trust in a relationship. And it's important to remember, as Abdoulah put it, "Not all customers are worth serving."

Of course, just as Abdoulah terminated that customer, she also had to fire employees from time to time. She came close to doing that with one of the key members of her team—only a month after he joined WOW!

She'd hired a new executive officer, a man we will call Bob, and discussed with him the company's culture and its core values: respect, accountability, integrity, and service (and recently, the company has added a fifth value, courage). He said he loved what he was hearing and talked enthusiastically about joining the company's Chicago-area office. About a month into his tenure, Abdoulah flew him to the Denver headquarters to meet with her in person. "So Bob comes into my office," she recalled, "and he's got a pad of paper listing all his accomplishments and the changes he's made. He said, 'I'm excited to be here, and I want to tell you how much we've done in the last month. I've got a list here we can go through.'"

Abdoulah wasn't interested. "No, that's not why you're here," she told him. "You're here because you may not be part of WOW!

for very long." Bob's jaw dropped, and his face turned ashen as he asked what she meant. "Let me tell you what I've heard about you: I've gotten a lot of feedback from your fellow employees," Abdoulah continued. "Yes, all the things you've done and the changes you've made are good, but you've done all of this in a way that is dictatorial, hierarchical, very autocratic, and micromanaged. You don't respond to email unless it's somebody with a title. You don't return calls in an appropriate amount of time. That's not what we do here. That's not how you serve your internal customer."

Bob just sat there and said, "You've heard all that just in the past thirty days?" Yes, she had, Abdoulah said and then asked, "What is it about the service structure that you don't get?" And he replied, "Let's go through it again."

So she led her wayward new executive through the company's service structure one more time and told him what it takes to lead in that kind of environment. And then he looked at her and said, "I got it. I intellectually understood the service structure and this culture before, but I had not embraced it in my heart and moved that intellectual knowledge into my behavior and into action." He stood up and said, "If you're comfortable with me, I'm ready to go now. I can tell you that you will never have to have this conversation with me or anyone on my team again." Abdoulah looked Bob in the eyes and said, "I trust that."

Recently, she told me, "Bob is one of the company's best leaders today." And one reason why he rose to the top stemmed from his CEO's strong leadership. At a fork in the road, where Bob could have been shown the path out of the company, Abdoulah applied WOW!'s core values to deal with him. She had the *courage* to confront him and the *integrity* to speak with him directly, face-to-face; she held him *accountable* for not treating his coworkers with *respect*; and she walked him through the service structure that made clear who she prioritized in her organization.

I wanted to know what motivated this dynamic, successful leader, so I asked Abdoulah the question I've been pondering for years and am addressing in this book. Are her actions—reining in her selfish ego when working alongside Terry, taking risks and the necessary time to investigate the cat situation, firing a customer, confronting a C-suite leader who was acting dictatorial, and other forms of behavior, policies, and decisions—are all of these seemingly self-sacrificial actions ultimately selfish? Because, in a profound way, they allow her to achieve so much success.

As a member of WOW's board of directors, I knew that Abdoulah had done very well financially and that she was a national icon in her industry. But I was curious to know if she felt that embracing the collective ego was a selfless or a selfish act.

"I believed so much in trying to foster a level of ownership at the frontline level and throughout the organization," she told me. "And I think this is a selfish approach, because I did it to create loyalty, to bring out a high degree of focus and a high level of ownership, and, if we had that in our organization, as an individual leader, I would absolutely benefit—not only operationally but financially. Also, I didn't ever want to take anything from this planet or that institution or any place with which I'm associated without feeling good about it. I must know that others have benefited too."

AFTER THE TAKEOVER: SUBJUGATING THE SELFISH EGO, SHUNNING THE C-SUITE, AND SETTLING NERVES

The temptations were intoxicating. I found myself listening to the seductive siren call of the sumptuous corner offices with their plush carpeting, mahogany desks, stocked refrigerators, and expensive artwork. My selfish ego constantly prodded me, like a devil's voice in my head, to compromise my leadership philosophy and move into an extravagant space. It seemed to whisper in my ears, "You deserve to be treated like who you are—the conquering CEO. To the victor go the spoils."

It's true that Integra Telecom and I were victorious. The year was 2007, and we'd just doubled the size of our company by acquiring one of our most competent competitors. For ten years, we'd been competing for customers and were both viewed as among the most successful companies in our industry. That multimillion-dollar buy-out, rewarding the company's management team and sharehold-ers with a fair price, was the culmination of a decade-long battle. We expected revenues to climb to more than $700 million annu-ally, with our client base stretching from our West Coast origins halfway across the continent to Minnesota, encompassing an elev-en-state region. We were poised for even greater success, and I felt the dizzying effects of triumph.

So maybe that voice was right: I *did* deserve to occupy the palatial C-suite.

It wasn't easy to keep myself out of those offices. In fact, it took several hours to convince my selfish ego that, in the long run, I'd be better off to reject the temptation to enjoy those decadent trap-pings. The collective ego prevailed, and I soon found myself in an uncomfortable environment. In the end, however, Integra Telecom would reap the benefits of my decision.

A Frightened Workforce

After the acquisition, I had come to Minneapolis, where the aquired company had been headquartered, and rented an apartment for two months. This allowed me to work at our newly acquired workplace during the business week (I'd fly back to my family in Portland on the weekends) to help successfully integrate the two organizations and the combined 2,500-plus people. At Integra Telecom, we operated a very different model that required being close to the customer, and, at that time, I also needed to be close to these employees to help teach them our focused approach to top-shelf customer care. The firm operated a top-down model that centralized all the customer-care people on a vast floor of cubicles in the big drab building. The office space was a meandering relic of the 1960s, complete with sliding windows that actually opened, chrome trim accents, and those dials above the elevator doors that point to the floor where the elevator paused. The building covered an entire city block, and we occupied three floors, just above the coveted third-floor skyways that connect many buildings in downtown Minneapolis, allowing one to walk for miles indoors, sheltered from the harsh Minnesota winters.

When I arrived, the people inside this work space were worried about a lot more than the cold and icy winds that would come to the Twin Cities in a few months. They were on edge, frightened even, concerned for their livelihoods, their families. I couldn't blame them for that. After all, I had just announced the termination of more than five hundred jobs and the relocation of many functions to out-of-state offices. I had to make the layoffs to cut costs and streamline our operations, and I had to move people around to staff positions closer to the customers, in accordance with our local, service-focused business model. Yet I knew none of that mattered to these anxious people. I had already taken steps to reassure this jittery workforce that the terminations were done with, but I knew I had to do more.

Here's how we handled the unavoidable layoffs and employee communications. While my team hand-delivered individual employment status letters throughout the entire acquired company—the letters clearly stated whether a person was retained or laid off—I met with every Minneapolis employee. "The layoffs are over," I explained to everyone. "We're sad for our peers whose positions have been eliminated, but now you all know your status. There is nothing more to fear. We're done, and there will be no more terminations. Now we need to get about the business of serving our customers, winning against the competition, and building a great company."

Still, I was concerned that they wouldn't fully believe me. And frankly, if I were in their shoes, I'd be skeptical too. At the time, just months before the economy imploded, ushering in the Great Recession, a lot of corporate takeovers were occurring. It was quite common for the acquiring company to come in and deliver wave after wave of layoffs. So it was understandable that my new employees would view my reassurances suspiciously.

Walking the Floor—with Sweaty Palms

Consequently, I needed to keep trying to ease these staffers' fears. What's more, their anxiety was my anxiety. I worried that, collectively, the workforce was too distracted to do what I needed them to do: take care of all the new customers we acquired. At that time, our competitors had embarked on a feeding frenzy, circling our acquired customers, sensing our vulnerability, knowing that during this time of transition we'd be prone to dropping calls, getting bills wrong, and generally screwing up and losing customers. In the months following any sort of acquisition like ours, the competition really goes for the jugular. So I needed—or rather, the entire Integra Telecom community needed—these employees to shed their angst and offer the kind of high-quality customer care for which our company had become known.

To that end, I did two things that I think helped but that also, frankly, made me uncomfortable. First, I walked the floors of the building, meeting and talking with the frontline employees. That was extremely difficult for me. I'd awkwardly try to stimulate everyday conversation. "Is that your family in those pictures?" I'd ask. "So, are you a native Minnesotan?" Or I'd turn to inquiries about the job and company. "What is the most common question you're getting today from our customers?" Or "Do you think they're aware of the acquisition?" One in three of these conversational efforts resulted in excruciating silence as the employee I approached froze with anxiety, confusing my introverted discomfort with a form of standoffishness.

This, I'm afraid, is typical for me, because, in situations like these, I often get tense. I feel self-conscious. I worry that I'll get asked something I can't adequately respond to. I have this paranoia that people will talk behind my back. I don't like being the center of attention, with people looking at my behavior and digesting my every word, testing my intellect. I get nervous that I won't perform as well as I'd like to perform. My palms get sweaty. My breathing tightens. I catch myself sneaking glances at my watch and saying to myself, "Okay, I'm going to do this for another five minutes. That's it. Then I'm retreating to the safety of my office."

Even though these conversational walkabouts were a strain for me, I pushed myself to do them. And, thankfully, they paid off, because I began to connect with people and get a much better sense of how our new colleagues performed their jobs.

Which leads to the second decision I believe made a positive impact on the morale of the workforce. During the first couple of days in Minneapolis, I used a barren conference room as my office. But mostly I was attending meetings, handling a wide range of demands, and, of course, walking the floor. I'd look inside the cubicles and other spaces of the call center, where the rank-and-file handled customer inquiries, for a place where I would work during my stay in the Twin Cities. My plan was to set up shop next to these frontline folks, to listen and learn, and perhaps more importantly, to allow my own actions to demonstrate the value I placed on our employees and how they treated customers.

This decision to sit and work for eight to ten hours a day in the call center with these employees, who I didn't know and who looked at me with skeptical eyes, wasn't an easy one. Of course, my selfish ego tried to seduce me with its silky persuasion: *You don't have to be here, Dudley. You don't have to subject yourself to the awkwardness of the scrutiny of all of these unfamiliar people looking at you. You could seclude yourself in the privacy and comfort of the luscious corner office with its luxurious leather couches like most conquering CEOs would do. Come on, Dudley, we both know you like such creature comforts.*

It's true; I do. But the collective ego, being its staid, steady, and sensible self, argued the counterpoint for long-term success: *Dudley Slater, CEO of Integra Telecom, you're making an investment in people. You need these employees to take care of twice as many customers as you used to have, twice as many calls coming in every day. You and this company can't succeed without the complete buy-in of this important workforce, which, as you know, is very skittish right now. They've seen hundreds of their coworkers get laid off in the last week because of the immediate need to combine these two companies. They're worried that those terminations were just the first dominoes to fall and that you're here to do nothing more than make some secret list of the next round of layoffs. If you just go sit in the prior CEO's corner office, you're allowing all of that employee anxiety to feed on itself and grow to become a crippling fear in this workforce.*

But the collective ego wasn't done yet: *On the other hand, Dudley, you have a real opportunity to roll up your sleeves and demonstrate, through your own actions and the way in which you spend your time, that the most important thing right now is to take care of the customers. If you're working shoulder to shoulder with the people in this apprehensive call center, you'll send the right message. That's the most important thing you can do right now as the CEO. So, about those desires you have for short-term comfort and pleasure: Get over it!*

That's a forceful argument. Case closed. Decision made.

Meeting Janet

Essentially, I was using those first couple of days to shop for the right person to share a space with—ideally, someone sitting in the busiest and most visible section of the building, someone who I sensed was committed to customers, someone who had the respect of his or her peers. So, with sweaty hands and brow, I walked and talked a lot during this time.

And then I met a colleague I will call Janet.

Janet's work area was in the busiest section of the floor, with pictures of her children on her desk. She's a lovely middle-aged woman with close-cropped dark hair and compassionate eyes behind sensible glasses. She exudes warmth and sincerity but also strength and confidence. She's the type of person who looks you in the eye. I could tell that she commanded respect. She'd been with the company for a long time, and I could see that she was a leader on this floor. I was drawn to her.

After talking to Janet for a while, I pointed to the workspace next to her and asked, "Is anyone using this space?" She told me it was available. "Good," I said. "I'm going to work here."

The look on her face said, *What did I just hear? You . . . work there? What are you talking about?* While many of the Minneapolis people were afraid of my presence because they thought I was there to determine who would get the axe next, Janet wasn't afraid. She was, however, confused.

And I felt I should help clear up her confusion. But I couldn't tell her that my leadership philosophy instructs me that where I spend my time is my way of messaging to everyone that *you guys are important.* That explanation would appear too manipulative.

What I did say was "Janet, our customers are the most important thing to this company. They're so important that I want to be here so I can hear, on a firsthand basis, what they're concerned about. I want to know why they're calling in. I want to know if you have the tools you need to be responsive to customers; if we, as an organization, have done everything we can to make you succeed. That's why I'm here. If I don't sit here and spend some real time with you and your team, I'll never know that."

Janet raised a wary eyebrow. She kept an open mind, but I'm sure she maintained her doubts about me and my positioning— right . . . next . . . to . . . her. Like many others I'd met when I roamed the workplace, she said, "I've never even met the previous CEO," and I bet she also thought, although she didn't say it, *much less have him sit next to me all day long.*

We're All Human

The rapport between Janet and me developed slowly. She had enough life experience so that she didn't take my word as the gospel truth. Her attitude reminded me of the Missouri motto: "Show me." But I didn't feel that she was closing me off at all; like I said, she had an open mind. I'd try to have fun with her and win her over with my dry sense of humor, but sometimes maybe my jokes were too dry for her or just plain not funny. The important thing, though, is that we got to know each other—more as peers than as a CEO and an employee—and when you're working with someone like that all day, they see you get up to go to the bathroom. They see you take a phone call from your wife to discuss the plumbing problem that happened that morning.

Because we were located in a very visible area, the other employees saw me too. They saw that I ate Subway sandwiches just like they did. They saw me as a human being. It's kind of like a kid who sees his teacher outside of school, like in a store, shopping: *Mrs. Johnson has to eat, too?!* This was important because while I wanted to gather information and see the operations firsthand as I worked on the floor, it was more about the employees seeing me, and ideally modeling my behavior.

Over the past decade, Janet and her colleagues rarely interacted with the members of the previous management team, because the senior leaders worked in a separate executive suite behind security doors with controlled access. That corner loomed in stark contrast to the utilitarian surroundings where Janet and her colleagues toiled away in dreary little cubicles. Once I arrived, the C-suites sat vacant, without movement or any sign of human activity.

The activity, the real action, was in the call center, where I learned a lot from Janet. Often, I felt the information exchange was one-way. She was educating me, and she didn't get a lot in return. But after weeks of this, she shared something with me that I could act on, an opportunity to fill a void we had in the way we trained new employees. With the previous company, Janet and her peers had worked on developing a web-based training package, and I wasn't aware it even existed. I stumbled into a conversation about that package, asked to see it, and saw a demo about it. I loved it. I got on the phone with our chief information officer and the vice president of human resources and said, "This is something we should use." Within a month, we rolled it out across the entire company, and it ended up saving us time and resources.

What Janet and her peers learned from that experience was *What they do matters.* They went outside of their job description to tell me that we could make the company better. They saw the CEO hear something and then do something about it that changed the company. That means you as an employee are not just punching the clock. You're a contributing member of something larger than yourself, and that's the linchpin in satisfying the hunger to find meaning in our work.

The experience changed Janet's and my relationship, too. I could tell from the way she started behaving, the way she greeted me, the way she began talking to me. The level of our mutual respect skyrocketed. And, although she never said so, I knew she was very proud about her pivotal role in the training package.

Enthusiasm Rippling Outward

Janet went on to work successfully with her team year after year, influencing new employees, her peers in Minneapolis, and, later, when she moved to a management role in California, all of those she supervised and worked with there. (By the way, I didn't have anything to do with her promotion; she earned it on her own.) She became a strong advocate for the company's model and operating philosophy of providing superior, local customer service. I suspect Janet touched more than a hundred people with her passion and professionalism. And I'd like to think those people went out and touched others among their circle of influence, and on and on, like a positive and human chain reaction. I truly do believe that a single inspired and committed member of an organization can—as his or her energy and enthusiasm reverberates outward—influence the entire organization, creating a far-reaching commitment to a cause or vision. Over time, this social-synergistic process fuels the collective ego and defines a company's culture.

In Integra Telecom's case, the heart of our culture and the most viable and sustainable path to long-term success was our dedication to offering the customer a unique human experience by establishing and nurturing trust, confidence, and long-term loyalty.

That human experience doesn't happen unless you've got front-line employees who are committed to making the customers' experience better than they could get anywhere else in the marketplace. This requires a willingness to go the proverbial extra mile, to make a commitment to listening, to following through. It's tempting, as a customer-care representative, to hang up the phone after hearing a customer's problems and think someone else in the organization will solve that issue. That kind of thinking goes like this: *All I have to do is open a work order, push a button, send it, and it will get taken care of.*

But you need to inspire that employee to initiate the work order and then invest the time to make a call two days later to see how that order is going, make sure that the unique customer concern has been taken care of, and then call the customer and say, "I followed up for you. Here's how your problem is being fixed . . . "

I saw Janet doing that and teaching that to her team in Minneapolis, and then even more so when she became a manager in California. You can't buy that. You can't give someone a 20 percent raise and expect he or she will do that. The person will be grateful for the raise and work hard for a month or two, and then the new normal sets in. The money doesn't give them the motivation to follow up, to truly care. What creates that is the satisfaction someone like Janet receives when she makes an investment in the customer and when the customer acknowledges it. That's special. We as human beings thrive on those special little moments in our relationships with other people; sometimes it's as simple as an unexpected smile from a stranger, a compliment from a friend, a handshake that matters, or a sincere thank-you from someone you've helped out. Colleen Abdoulah certainly prioritized these magical points in time by chronicling her organization's WOW! Moments.

If Janet sees from me that those special moments are valued in this company and that the CEO is going to give you the tools to create those moments, she's going to be energized by it. And she did just that. By my willingness to stay and work in Minneapolis—ignoring the allure of the posh C-suite—and invest my time with the frontline people and with customers, she saw what I valued. That gave her the validation and confidence that she would be valued if she did the same.

By the time I left Minneapolis, the fear and anxiety among the employees had been replaced by a sense of accountability, a pride in offering something that no other telecommunications company was offering, and a sense of ownership over the relationship between that workforce and their customers. As a result, sales in the Minnesota market soared, and Integra Telecom continued to succeed.

The demands of integrating a $700-million acquisition and its employees initially required me to spend substantially all my time with other executives, which offered an easier, commonly followed management path. After an internal struggle, I realized I needed to spend time on the floor and not tucked safely away in a luxurious office. I needed to make a decision on who to prioritize within the organization and where to set up my workspace in that Minneapolis building. Suffice it to say, I'm glad the collective ego won the argument.

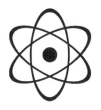

CHAPTER 2

WHO LEAVES YOUR MEETING AS THE SMARTEST PERSON IN THE ROOM?

NO ONE SAID IT'D BE EASY: THE CRITICAL TOOL OF LEARNING TO SHUT UP, LISTEN, AND ADJUST

As the CEO of Zulily, one of the twenty-first century's fastest-growing, most successful online retail businesses, Darrell Cavens knows how to motivate and push his workforce to meet the ever-increasing demand for the company's wide range of products—from baby clothes to home decor. He also knows how to pull back. He understands that sometimes and with some people, hard-charging leaders have to calibrate the situation, adjust their style, and throttle down. (Incidentally, in 2015, QVC bought Zulily for $2.4 billion.)

He didn't always know this. He learned it through a no-nonsense—even brusque—directive hurled his way.

In the mid-1990s, Cavens worked for a Seattle firm called Starwave, a producer of online content sites created by Microsoft cofounder Paul Allen. The company provided such terrific material for outlets like ESPN SportsZone and ABCNews.com that Disney acquired it for $350 million—a fair piece of change for a start-up in that era. "We had a very talented group of people who were engaged in doing some amazing projects," Cavens told me.

One day, his boss sat him down for a performance review, looked him in the eyes, and said, "'You're clearly one of the smartest guys in the room, but you'd be able to get so much more done if you'd just shut up from time to time and listen to what other people have to say,'" Cavens recalled. "That was one of those wake-up calls, where you're like, 'Uh . . . okay.'"

Stunned, Cavens zombie-walked back to his office, initially reacting the way most people would, saying to himself, "Did he really just say that to me? That's horrible feedback. How do I internalize that?"

But it didn't take him long to realize that the brutally honest assessment was spot-on. "It was some of the best feedback I ever received," he said. "You think you're doing things the right way and contributing to the team, and then you get smacked upside the head. It was one of those moments in my career when I said to myself, *Wow, there really is a different and better way.* I took that to heart from that point on."

He learned to sit back a little more during meetings, let other people talk, and help guide the conversation rather than forcefully lead it. And to this day, he continues to do that. "That guidance-versus-leading approach has served me incredibly well, because, so often, folks have these incredible ideas that are much smarter than what I'd be able to come up with," Cavens said.

While a firm-but-helpful boss taught Cavens to do this relatively early in his career, I had to be pulled aside later in my career, after I was already CEO. More on my journey later. Even after I changed my approach, I still had to remind myself to step back from time to time. I asked Cavens if he found it—and maybe still does find it—difficult to allow other people to be the smartest in the room. "Do you ever feel," I asked, "like you'd love to set the person straight or are certain that you could get the idea across better? Do you ever struggle with that?"

Here's what he said: "Yes, it's an interesting situation. Often, you feel like you know the answer and ask yourself, 'Why can't people figure this out? They might if I just jump in here.' But sometimes you come to realize, later, that you didn't know the answer, that there's something better out there. When that happens a couple of times, you tend to be more open about it. But yes, I struggle and wonder why other people don't understand what I understand. It's important to realize that there's a participatory benefit we get from having different viewpoints. And yet it's like learning not to follow your instincts. You need to sit back and include others in that decision process. It's not always intuitive to do that."

On the other hand, sometimes you do need to interrupt someone during a meeting to ensure that no one person dominates. "And that means that, when needed, I have to step in, stop somebody, and say, 'Why don't you let Sally talk for a minute?'" Cavens said. "I used to be that somebody who should have been stopped during a meeting. Now I try to help the other folks around the room engage."

Of course, you can't effectively play that role—the one who reins in the guy or gal who babbles on and on—unless you've laid the groundwork and cultivated a reputation as someone who embraces inclusive debate. Cavens has done just that. "I think I've got a style that's very collaborative and open so when I do have to interrupt somebody during a meeting, people are like, 'Oh yeah.' What I've found is that five other people in the room usually feel grateful: 'Thank goodness Darrell has stepped in.' We've all been in that meeting before, where somebody just won't shut up. They push the same message over and over again, and the other team members usually don't want to say anything because this person has the loudest voice. So others often feel the same way, but nobody has the gumption to tell that person to stop."

I've tried to guide meetings in the same way, redirecting the conversation away from the dominating voice and toward the rest of the people at the table. And you have to do it in a very respectful way. Cavens said he'll communicate something like this: *I understand your point, and I'd love to get some different opinions.* "Depending on the person," he said, "that will often shut them down. Later, I will try to reengage them back in. It's a challenge of the CEO role."

Embracing Contrasts in Brainstorming Styles

Another related challenge inherent in Fusion Leadership surfaces when one of your team members processes information and generates ideas more slowly than you do, walks when you want to run, ruminates and digests when you want to gobble and go. Many CEOs believe the person with the more deliberate style slows down the team and therefore demand that he or she learn to pick up the pace or be left behind and shown the door. Fusion Leaders refute that assumption and avoid losing a potentially talented team member.

In 2010, when Cavens was first getting Zulily off the ground, he noticed that one of his management team members constantly exhibited that go-slow behavior, which stood in sharp contrast to the rip-roaring, movin'-and-shakin' style of Cavens and most of the other decision makers at the company. This employee, who I'll call Jennifer, simply thought and acted at a more measured pace, which Cavens initially misinterpreted, considering her one-baby-step-at-a-time mode a weakness.

"In the early days of the business, I would say, 'Here's this great idea. Let's go run with it,'" he recalled. "But Jennifer would pause and look across the table and say, 'Well, I don't know about that. I have to think about it.' At first, I very much took that as a fault: She wasn't catching on to what I was thinking and wasn't keeping up. In hindsight, I realized it was a huge mistake on my part to make that assumption."

Such reflective and deliberate methodology contrasts with the run-and-gun line of attack taken by Cavens and many other corporate leaders, especially those operating in cutting-edge technology markets, like Zulily. Slowly, however, Cavens noticed that when Jennifer had some space and time to ponder a problem, she'd often come back with an innovative solution. "She'd return in a day or two and say, 'Why don't we try this?' And I'd say, 'Oh my god, that's brilliant!'"

But it took a few instances like this before it really resonated with Cavens that he needed to adapt to her style. Over the course of a few days in 2011, his full understanding of her approach gelled, and then, suddenly, he got it.

"The first time this really hit me was when we were doing an organizational design exercise," he said. "We were looking at her team, which had doubled or tripled in size, and we had not reworked the management structure at all. So people were starting to have twenty direct reports; at some point, that becomes moderately dysfunctional. So we were wondering if we should organize this by the type of job somebody's doing or by the divisions they're going after or by something else entirely. Do we organize this into teams, where they group together across different functional elements? We were up at the whiteboard looking at all these things."

Cavens and some members of the leadership group brainstormed several organizational structures, and his instinct directed him to draw up one flow chart and "drive to an action plan," as he put it. The group considered various options, but after two hours, they'd run out of time for the day without a satisfactory result.

Consequently, Caven's reflective colleague Jennifer had the chance to mull over a few ideas and think about the problem in detail. "She came back in with a different approach and some thoughtful ideas on what different people we could put in these roles and what skill sets mattered," he said. "It got us to a very quick answer. After two hours of us going in circles in our last session, she went off on her own, thought about the problem, and when we reconvened in a few days, she outlined a model that was different from what we had drawn up on the whiteboard. We showed our enthusiasm for her fantastic idea, went with it, and it still serves as the organizational design we're using today."

When Cavens and his team saw her new problem-solving organizational structure laid out on the whiteboard, that's when he fully understood the value his colleague could bring to the conference room when she was given the space and time to brainstorm alone and in her own way. Just as important, he also made a commitment to himself to adapt to her style of working—and others' as well. "It was one of those light bulb moments, when I realized I need to work differently with her," he said. "It reminded me that you have to look around at the team and realize others probably also have different ways of working and thinking. I ended up being a better leader after that, simply by being aware."

Radiating Outward and into the Workforce

Now, don't think such a managerial transformation goes unnoticed. Jennifer, the woman with the solution, may not have completely grasped Caven's internal adjustment, but she did welcome his appreciation of her idea and also responded with a renewed sense of on-the-job fulfillment. Is it a stretch to say she exuded satisfaction after her partners embraced her idea?

"No, it's absolutely not a stretch to say that," Caven's said. "She demonstrated a confidence I hadn't seen before. She felt good that she found a complex system solution to the problem as opposed to a bunch of gobbledygook thoughts coming out of my mouth."

What's more, the passion she exhibited from her success undoubtedly radiated outward to others at Zulily, fusing together a stronger workplace nucleus, if you will. Cavens's enthusiastic reaction to her solution cemented her loyalty to him and the company.

This isn't the only example of Cavens pulling back his natural instincts—not to mention his need for speed; Zulily's a fast-moving company that generally encourages fluidity and quick thinking—to advance the organization's mission. He does whatever he can to nurture a collaborative and respectful culture, one that allows for different styles and leaves room for diverse thinking. And that doesn't happen if you rush to solve every issue your way.

"There's a respect for ideas that's hard to get if you run over the conversation," he said. "I think [Jennifer] and other folks have been extremely loyal because I truly care about their thoughts. People open up so much more when you sometimes sit on your hands and keep your mouth shut. I so often learn things this way, and I'm able to dig into a set of questions that leads to me learning an incredible amount of information. And they feel like I care—because I do. You can't fake this stuff. You've got to be genuinely interested."

The Proof Is in the Proverbial Pudding

Now, all of this pull-back strategy—or, put another way, *managerial retrenchment*—falls flat without tangible results. And sure enough, it's impossible not to see triumph in Zulily's numbers. This brand of Fusion Leadership has paid and continues to pay dividends to the company and its employees. Of course, it also benefits its CEO, who, by the way, is an Ernst & Young National Entrepreneur of the Year Award winner. Consider this record of success:

Since launching the company in January 2010 with ten employees, Cavens and his leadership team have significantly grown their ranks and revenues and as of late 2014 had 1,900 employees, plus another four thousand warehouse associates who are not all officially their employees—yet. In 2014, Zulily had $1.2 billion in sales. "And we do that $1.2 billion in sales $18 at a time, because the average item we sell is $18, and our average order is $55," Cavens said. "It's a volume business." That's for sure!

Zulily is headquartered in Seattle, but the company keeps outgrowing its office space, and the Seattle employees are now working out of their sixth office in four and a half years. Cavens and his organization have another corporate office in Columbus, Ohio, with 150 employees, and one in London with sixty employees. They also have a distribution center in Reno, Nevada, as well as one in Columbus. Each of those centers is about 700,000 square feet. That's over sixteen acres under one roof. From one end to the other, the building covers about a third of a mile—a very busy third of a mile. "There's a tremendous amount of motion and movement in the buildings," Cavens said.

Zulily has grown both quickly and extensively. "We are in rare company with folks like Amazon and Gap in terms [of the pace of sales and growth]," he said. "It's interesting when my team and I are going over forecasts that have incredibly large numbers, and the team doesn't look at me and say, 'You're absolutely nuts.' Although, they may be thinking that. This year, we will add over 500 million in sales dollars gross this year. That's more than the total size of the business two years ago; so it's considerably larger."

Cavens is also clearly proud of the diversity within his workforce: "We have the software engineer with twenty-five years of experience and the high school grad who's joining us for his or her first job. And we have everything in between."

Cavens tries as best he can to connect with those employees on a very real, down-to-earth level, which means, among other things, that he reminds himself to pump the brakes on a natural tendency that most leaders share. That is, as CEO of Integra Telecom, I had to understand that I could squash people so quickly and so unintentionally and not even realize I was doing it. Fusion Leaders often have to subjugate their seat-of-the-pants propensity to march to the front of the room, grab the marker from the whiteboard, and take over. It's a strong temptation to resist.

What you're communicating when you force yourself to stay in your chair is your desire to foster that culture of mutual respect, one that encourages open debate. It's what allows people to feel comfortable coming forward. It opens the door for success and begs the question: Who leaves your meetings as the smartest person in the room?

CONFRONTATION AT THE CROSSROADS: A SIMPLE FIX CAN REIGNITE WORKFORCE COMMITMENT

We've all fallen victim to The Interrupter, the person who, for various reasons, such as a sense of power, urgency, or entitlement, won't let you finish your sentence. He cuts you off and plows ahead with his own thoughts, which he apparently feels are far more important than yours. While many of these people interrupt intentionally, others are clueless. They barge right into the conversation, verbally stepping over you, without the slightest idea that they're being rude. Either way, it's an annoying habit. I should know. I was that guy, and I knew I was doing it: I was The Intentional Interrupter.

In 2000, relatively early during my time as CEO of Integra Telecom and four years after I cofounded the company, I routinely felt a burning desire to demonstrate that I was the smartest person in the room. My individual ego needs nearly cost me and the organization all that we'd gained.

My team and I had just taken Integra Telecom to the next level. We'd raised more than $200 million, which was, at the time, the largest private capital financing in Oregon's history, according to *The Oregonian* newspaper. And we were aiming for more.

It was a new century, we were riding high, and I was an early-forties CEO who had really gotten the company's momentum going. I was extremely focused on my relationships with the private-equity investors backing our company and growth. We'd fly them in from the East Coast and Texas to our offices in Portland, where they'd sit in on our board meetings and ask all kinds of pointed and challenging questions about the business. After all, they wanted assurance they were backing the right company, with the right team.

Usually, our entire executive team would attend these meetings, providing a lot of potential brainpower. Yet when the investors would ask their hard questions, I often found myself dominating the discussion, even though their queries might be answered better by someone else. I felt a dire need to prove my worth as CEO, to show these fat-cat financiers my intelligence and command of the company.

This is when I became The Intentional Interrupter, especially to an employee I'll call Tom, a senior officer who was responsible for major portions of our company's technology. I'd cut him off at every turn in his conversation with the investors. I knew exactly why I was doing it and *thought* I was smart to do it. But I was wrong.

In the telecommunications arena, there's no more crucial area than the network. The telecom landscape is littered with companies that made bad decisions about how they built their networks. They put in the wrong equipment or installed devices that weren't compatible with other devices or invested in equipment that didn't deliver what the customer needed. You can make horrible mistakes in dozens of ways as you're constructing these very expensive systems (we would ultimately spend billions of dollars on our network). And you can only afford to construct it once. If you make a mistake building your network, you've blown it. Your business is dead on arrival.

Tom was an essential, irreplaceable member of our team. His technological expertise was crucial to the success of the company as we worked hard to serve our customers and grow Integra Telecom in a fiercely competitive market. If your telecom company lacks a passionate, committed network expert like Tom—well—it's unlikely you will last long. If I were to make a list of the people I would most want to inspire to come to work every Monday morning with fire in their belly and the desire to make the company succeed, it would start with the people in technology.

Tom had that fire.

He was also tremendously knowledgeable about engineering, which is obviously an area vital to the success of a company like Integra Telecom. Now, I have a scientific background—I started my career as a geophysicist at Texaco—and I try to stay informed on the latest developments in the engineering field. But Tom will read more in a year about this subject than I'll read in a lifetime. His expertise runs deep. I can think of many times when I'd read something about a new technological innovation and say to myself, *Oh my god, this is so fundamental to our business*, and race down to Tom's office. I'd ask him, "Tom, are you aware of this new development in IP engineering?" I was nervous that we weren't staying current.

But he'd always put my mind at ease as he pulled out stacks of materials he'd been reading and say something like, "We've been on this for months, and this is why we made the decision to buy this type of gear."

I would walk out of there feeling so relieved because I'd rushed into his office in a panic, worrying that the entire house would collapse, and I'd come out of his office realizing we'd built such a solid foundation beneath the house that we didn't have to worry about it.

Rewarding My Ego While Losing Tom

Tom was a very thorough and thoughtful person. His depth of knowledge about technological issues was astounding, and he wasn't comfortable giving a simple answer unless it was qualified with the proper context, all the underlying principles and premises that got him to the answer. Put another way: If you asked him what time it was, he'd tell you how to make a watch.

And therein lies the reason why I interrupted him in those board meetings. An investor who knew finances inside and out but understood virtually nothing about the intricacies of our company's technology would raise an issue, and Tom would say, "Well that's an interesting question, and its answer requires some context." He'd then start to offer a deliberate-as-the-day-is-long monologue studded with arcane engineering and technical jargon.

I would get incredibly impatient—and worried because I saw the investors' blank faces and empty stares as Tom added detail after detail. So when he'd start to get deep into talking about "multiplexing equipment" or "data transmission speeds" or "IP backplanes," I'd cut him off in midsentence. Because of my technical experience, I knew the answer to the question and also knew the investors didn't want a soliloquy on IP switching technology or whatever. They wanted a succinct explanation, in layman's terms.

And frankly, I must say, the investors loved my answers. I knew enough about the topic to be credible, and I saved them the inconvenience, or drudgery, of listening to a long, overly detailed technical answer. I made the decision to serve the interests of the investors, and in so doing, I was increasing my own stock and reputation in the eyes of these financial heavyweights; they'd openly compliment my straightforward answers. But as a result, I was annoying, even angering, and certainly alienating Tom.

This didn't happen just once or even a few times. It became my pattern of behavior over the course of months. Consequently, Tom became increasingly detached, and I'd even notice that he'd leave those meetings dejected, his shoulders slumped, his head hanging down. But I didn't connect the dots. It didn't register within me that my actions were the direct cause of his melancholy.

Here's why he was so distraught. The signal I was communicating to Tom each time I cut him off was *I don't trust what you're about to say* or *I don't value your participation in this dialogue.* And those are such negative messages. How could he not conclude that I was undermining him? He'd be explaining something quite well, albeit methodically, and then someone who was less knowledgeable than him would stampede all over his explanation and offer up a short, succinct answer to the question. So what had been a dialogue between an investor and Tom shifted and became a dialogue between the investor and me, shutting Tom out.

What's more, the eye contact would be redirected as well. The investors would turn their attention and gazes to me. It used to be (and maybe to a lesser extent still is the case) that if I wasn't getting enough eye contact, I'd start to feel insecure. By interrupting Tom, I'd feel more secure—at his expense. In retrospect, I completely understand why he felt so dejected.

Although I didn't know it, the real problem for me, and more importantly, for the organization, was that I was losing Tom.

Killing Conversations and Creating a Clock Puncher

Tom and I had known each other for many years; we'd worked together at another company and become friends. But I noticed, after a few months of the meetings, he stopped inviting me to go fishing with him, an activity we'd previously enjoyed together. When I'd walk into his office and he was talking to some of his subordinates, the conversation would stop. Months prior to that, I would walk in and just become a part of the conversation. But that changed. I became the killer of conversations. The silence was awkward and the mood glum.

I started seeing tangible evidence that Tom was becoming detached from me and, therefore, detached from Integra Telecom. After a few months of being trampled on during those meetings, he was halfway out the door, if not from a career standpoint, at least from a commitment perspective. He was on the cusp of transforming from a passionate member of the team to a clock puncher.

And we couldn't afford to have any clock punchers, not in that tough, competitive business, and especially not in a role that was as important as Tom's.

To put it simply: I flat-out screwed up because I needed to prove my intelligence during those meetings as a way of addressing my own insecurities and feeding my individual ego. I nearly messed up the whole company, too, because I'm convinced that Tom would have left Integra Telecom had I not changed my behavior. . . . But I did.

I'd like to say that, being an enlightened and strategic corporate leader, I saw the error of my ways and corrected my behavior on my own. But I was too obtuse at the time to see all of this. It took someone else to point it out.

One day, after a board meeting, with the investors out of the building and on their way to the airport, the management team members finished our usual post–meeting wind-down with a little debriefing, a few jokes, and a sense of relief and accomplishment. (Those meetings were often high-wire stress scenes, and we were glad when they concluded.) After our chill-out session, I walked to my office and sat down. Within seconds, it seemed, Jim, our chief operating officer at the time, stormed into my office.

Voice raised and clearly angry, Jim confronted me. "Damn it, Dudley! Why do you always do that to Tom?" he said, pounding his fist on a table. "Why do you treat him like that?"

"Do what to Tom?" I said. "Treat him like what? What are you talking about?"

"You cut him off in conversation, all the time, like he's a misdirected schoolboy and you're the all-knowing teacher," Jim said, or words to that effect. He went on to tell me that my interruption pattern had been manifesting for months, that I interrupted others, too, but not as often as I did Tom, and that my domineering behavior was messing with Tom's psyche, diminishing his performance, and dulling his commitment to the company.

I was stunned by the confrontation. Jim was perhaps my greatest mentor and later became one of my closest friends. And I immediately knew his accusation was right! It suddenly became very clear to me that I had to break my habit of cutting Tom off. I had to get him back. We were at the crossroads, and I had to take the right path.

So I changed my style. I started letting him answer questions—thoroughly. I realized that *sometimes it pays to shut up*, as John Baldoni once wrote in *Forbes* magazine, regarding the desire to come across as the most intelligent person in a meeting. It was really a very simple adjustment to stop interrupting Tom, express appreciation for his answers, and compliment him on his thoroughness. I started directing questions to him. Someone would ask me a technical question, and I would turn and say, "Tom, why don't you answer that, because you know more about this topic than I do."

As it turns out, building him up was easy. These board meetings happened once a quarter, and I came to understand that if a meeting took an extra ten minutes—well, so what? In the greater scheme of things, it wasn't that big a deal. But Tom's well-being was a big deal.

Small Change, Big Results

As I reflect on this, I wish I would've always let Tom go on and answer a question in his long-winded way, even if it created a sense of impatience in myself and the investors. I could've always circled back to them later to tell them why it was good for them, and the company, to listen to Tom's time-consuming explanations. That would have sent Tom the right message: *You're valuable. You're the most knowledgeable person in this meeting as it relates to these engineering issues. And we need you.* Instead, I'd been sending the opposite message and, consequently, exercising the opposite of bringing the organization together and practicing Fusion Leadership, a philosophy I was still several years away from fully embracing.

I came within an eyelash of losing Tom. But thanks to Jim's figurative punch to my face and a very subtle, small change in my leadership style and my understanding of what motivated him, Tom was rejuvenated. His confidence grew and our relationship blossomed.

He started coming into my office to talk, confiding in me, and (I write this with a smile) asking me to go fishing with him again.

Tom stayed with Integra Telecom for another eleven years, and, most importantly, he became a champion of the company. He exuded a positive attitude, expected excellence from his people, and held them accountable while treating them in a way that inspired them. They, in turn, fed off his energy. His renewed commitment created a current, traveling outward, connecting people and their ideas and dedication like an incredibly interwoven electrical network. Because he was so positive about the company, he became a spokesman of sorts for Integra Telecom's mission. By encouraging one strong advocate in Tom, I actually ended up with hundreds of advocates, because they were all the people within his circle of influence at the company.

I tell this story because Fusion Leadership is all about relationships and how our interactions with other people can yield results that benefit the entire organization. Through nurturing the collective ego for the greater good in the long term, we also reward our own individual egos.

I can't overstate the impact we all felt within the company because of one seemingly subtle behavior alteration that brought a vital team member back from the brink of departure. Tom led the entire team that constructed the network we needed, allowing Integra Telecom to avoid the mistakes that unraveled some of our competitors. Unlike those who did make missteps, we never had to write off millions of dollars of capital because we put the wrong devices in the network. We never had to explain to our customers why we didn't have an elaborate, effective network. The ultimate consequences of one decision—*let Tom talk*—were enormous and far-reaching. Our passion-filled technology and engineering teams were one of the most important reasons why Integra Telecom grew to become, as quantified by many, one of the most successful companies in its industry nationally.

To this day, I shudder to think that I was so close to draining the enthusiasm and commitment out of such a vital cog in the Integra Telecom wheel. Yet, it took just a simple adjustment to a bad habit—the effects of which I hadn't realized until I was confronted about it. I would go so far as to say that that specific change, by itself, easily could have been the difference between success and failure for the entire company. Without a dedicated and passionate technological expert at the network helm, Integra Telecom could've been lost. Fortunately, by changing my behavior, I was able to change our organization's trajectory. It was a simple yet powerful fix.

CHAPTER 3

HOW DO YOU
DELIVER BAD NEWS?

MAKING IT PERSONAL: THE NAME,
THE FACE, AND THE BAD NEWS

In the late 1970s, flight attendant Jeff Pinneo was welcoming passengers onboard a Continental Airlines flight to Houston when the company's vice president walked down the jetway, held out his hand to Pinneo, and said, "Hi, Jeff. I'm Charlie Bucks. How are you?"

It was a simple greeting, but it meant a lot to Pinneo. At the time, he was just three years into what would become a three-decades-long career in the airline industry, where he would eventually become CEO of Horizon Air. The only connection the popular and charismatic Continental VP had to Pinneo came from a letter of recommendation that a friend of Pinneo's father had sent to Bucks, praising the young man and saying he'd be a good hire. Bucks wrote a letter back to the family friend, closing with this line: "If Jeff's everything you say he is, we certainly have got to give him a good look." Evidently, they did look, liked what they saw, and hired the kid, who was working his way through college.

Pinneo received a copy of Bucks's letter, which was written on gold-embossed Continental stationery. "I still have it," he said. So why did the encounter mean so much to him? Why does Pinneo get a little misty-eyed when he recounts the story? It's because the executive took the time to find out who was working the flight, remembered the young flight attendant from that letter, and, in a gesture that particularly struck a chord with Pinneo, Bucks used his name: "Hi, Jeff."

"From that point on, the power of name recognition has resonated with me," Pinneo said, recalling the importance of that simple moment at the dawn of his professional career and how it represents something much deeper. "Through the course of their lives, people identify with many things, and it's important to key in on that. For some, it's family or tradition or ethnic heritage. But for a lot of people, it's the company that they work for and, perhaps above all else, their own name."

During his 2002–2010 tenure as the leader of Horizon, Pinneo worked hard to remember the names of his employees so he could greet them personally. His success had more to do with his habit of review than a photographic memory. "I probably get way more credit for having a good memory for names than really I do," he said. "I had a science behind it. It was preparation going in. I would say, 75 percent of the time, it was just straight memory, but 25 percent of the time, it was a function of where I was going to be and who was going to be there. It required deliberate preparation. And often, beyond the name, other things about the people would flow out too—their situation, their family, their kids, their health, that kind of stuff. It's a big company—about four thousand people—but not so big that you couldn't do that."

Pinneo would use those names as he walked through an airport, past ticket counters and boarding gates, greeting Horizon people with "Hi, Margaret" and "How are you, Dan?" and "Nice to see you, Karen." I have no doubt that Margaret, Dan, and Karen appreciated that their boss recognized them. I tried to do the same thing when I was at Integra Telecom. Before I'd go visit a service office, I'd have the human resources department print out the names and pictures of all of the employees at that location so I could study them on the flight out. It doesn't sound like much, but using people's names makes a huge impact. And it's really not that hard to do. That is, you can get a lot of bang for your buck.

Pinneo tells me that he "absolutely" said hello to *all* of the Horizon employees he'd see as he walked down the concourse. "I had to build in an extra fifteen to twenty minutes on both ends of any trip," he said.

But that was all a part of constructing a culture at Horizon in which people were treated with respect, something he also did in his next position as the president and CEO of Medical Teams International, a Northwest-based nonprofit global health care and disaster relief organization. Creating and maintaining such a culture isn't always easy, but Fusion Leaders clearly understand that the right kind of work environment can foster the right kind of workforce—with people who are motivated and passionate about their jobs.

"Check Those Seat Pockets in Front of You"

Here's another way Pinneo demonstrated mutual respect as Horizon's leader. Whenever he'd fly and the plane landed, he'd wait for all the passengers to deplane so he could help the flight crew clean out the seat pockets, pick garbage up off the floor, and make sure the baggage bins were empty. Now, stop a minute and think about this. How do you feel when the plane has landed after a long flight—or even a short one—and the passengers are standing, getting their bags, and texting or calling on their smartphones? I know how I feel: I. Want. Off. The. Plane. Now. *Let's go, people!* I think *Move it along! I've got places to go and people to meet.*

Okay, let's add another layer to this scenario. You're the CEO of the airline. Wouldn't it be natural to feel entitled, that you should be among the first off the plane? I might. I certainly wouldn't want to hang around to pick up junk that other people left behind.

But not Jeff Pinneo. Sticking around to help clean was important, and despite really not wanting to do it sometimes, he felt he had very little choice in the matter. "If I didn't, even one time, word would spread among the Horizon community faster than anything on social media," he said. "So it didn't matter how busy

I was or what meeting I was trying to get to—I helped prepare the plane for its next flight. Culturally, that was something you could not miss. At Horizon, everybody did everything. For example, we had a very good pilot, one of our best, who wouldn't think twice about coming out on his days off to paint ground equipment, if that's what needed to be done. We had an entrepreneurial, we're-all-in-this-together understanding."

Pinneo led his company with the knowledge that, as CEO, virtually all of his actions were noticed and meant something to the workforce. "Everything you do is visible, and I can certainly affirm that people pay attention to everything," he said. "I have this rule of thumb that, from the time you walk out of the men's room stall, you're on the stage," he added with a chuckle. "You need to be aware—not to put on an act or anything—but just be aware that everything's messaging when you're CEO."

It's important to keep in mind the environment in which Pinneo found himself when he became CEO and to understand the extent to which he navigated the airlines around obstacles, over sinkholes, and to the top of the profession. He took the controls in January 2002 under the lingering cloud of the 9/11 attacks, with the entire airline industry hit hard by the fallout from that awful day. Many people were afraid to fly, and air travel became much more heavily regulated. In short, the world had changed dramatically, and no industry was more affected than the airline sector.

What's more, the public's perception of Horizon had been tainted since January 2000, when its parent company, Alaska Airlines, suffered its worst tragedy ever. On the last day of that month, Alaska Airlines Flight 261, bound for Seattle, plunged into the Pacific Ocean off the coast of California, killing all eighty-eight passengers and crew. Obviously, the disaster affected the entire corporation for years.

And let's not forget that the nation had been limping along economically during the recession of 2001, which carried serious ramifications for the airline industry and, as a short-haul regional business carrier, Horizon in particular.

In other words, Pinneo had his work cut out for him.

Tough Calls, Great Results

By exercising his distinct brand of Fusion Leadership, Pinneo made several difficult decisions that led to challenging but necessary and ultimately successful business moves. These included consolidating Horizon's airline fleet, negotiating with pilots, closing flight crew bases, and cancelling service to some cities, just to name a few.

Under his stewardship, Horizon grew its revenues from $415 million to over $720 million in 2007, increasing profitability in all but one of the years following 9/11. I mention the year 2007 because that's when the Horizon team won a prestigious global award from *Air Transport World* magazine, which named Horizon as its 2007 Regional Airline of the Year. In making its judgment, the review panel at *Air Transport World* considered a range of criteria, including business model innovation, financial performance, quality of service, and, importantly, corporate culture—yes, the panel reviewed and appreciated that supportive, respectful work environment Pinneo worked so hard to nurture and preserve.

While Pinneo gained a lot of praise within the profession for the award and the success it represented, he made sure others claimed some of the fame as well. At the awards banquet where Horizon collected its honor, the CEO brought enough employees with him to fill two large tables. "I had flight attendants, pilots, mechanics, and stock clerks, who were all able to be there to celebrate something that we considered extraordinary," he said.

In the Shoes of Others

Early in his tenure, due to tough economic conditions, Pinneo had to downgrade some pilots from high-level positions to lower ones and, consequently, furlough some junior staff members who were employed at the bottom of the workforce chain. While some of the employees affected heard the news from their supervisors, the pilots often met with Pinneo face-to-face. Frequently, he wanted to be the one to deliver the news—well, that's not exactly accurate; no one *wants* to deliver bad news. He felt, out of respect, he *should* be the person to tell the pilots about the changes he was forced to make for the good of the entire organization. The health of the company depended on these life-altering changes.

And they were, indeed, life-altering. Consider this: Those pilots had been first officers for a long time and then finally reached upgrade potential and became captains, moving from the right seat to the left. Now they were faced with a downgrade, the prospect of going back to the right seat. Such a move is a change in responsibility, authority, and pay. "So the news of that transition required special communication and attention to that group," Pinneo said.

He would approach such meetings with what he calls "strategic and intentional empathy." Although Pinneo is one of the most modest people I've ever met, he acknowledges that he's good—darn good—at vicariously projecting into another person's situation. When he goes to deliver bad news, he takes on a persona. It's not that he's acting or being disingenuous; he simply dials into his best empathetic state of mind, because he knows that the person or people he's meeting will be suffering. Yet he also reminds himself to stay on task.

Here's how he explained the role he'd step into: "Some of the same practices that apply when you go to meet with a grieving friend apply here. There's mourning going on. They're losing something, and if you use that analogy of a friend who has just lost a spouse or family member, you go through a cognitive reversal, an emotional reversal, before you go in to talk with the person. Before such an encounter, I spend a moment to project myself into their circumstances as best I can—to feel it: What would I be seeing? What would I be thinking? I want to get into their space deeply enough that my first actions are warm and empathetic. But I also know that I have a role of responsibility to help them connect with the realities. And there's also a boundary component to it. You can't get sucked so far into their grief that you're ineffective."

Often, Pinneo said, he begins a difficult conversation with sincere gratitude, offering thanks for the service the employees have performed during their time with the company. "I tell them, 'I appreciate you. I also appreciate what you must be going through. I know that this has got to be affecting you on a number of different levels, and I'm sorry about that. I wish it weren't so, but it is so for reasons I'll explain. How can I help you connect with this in a way that creates a pathway for you to see a way through it?'"

Pinneo believes—and I wholeheartedly agree—that if leaders can do this well, they can make tough decisions and act on them as gracefully as possible. In the end, such leadership helps steer organizations out of trouble and into a place where the group as a whole can succeed.

"Because It Mattered to Him"

Now, it's not that Pinneo would always meet face-to-face with the recipients of bad news; sometimes he'd send his lieutenants to do the difficult work. Like any leader, you have to prioritize your time and decide when something needs your personal attention. When I talked with him about this, Pinneo said he made that call after he determined if a decision carried "enterprise-wide materiality." If it did, he got directly involved. It also depended on who was on the bad end of a tough move.

For example, in about 2006, Pinneo and his leadership team concluded that, for financial reasons, they had to reduce the size of their airplane fleet, which meant phasing out some expensive, top-of-the-line, high-tech airplanes that many of the senior pilots loved. "They considered these planes their babies," he said.

Consequently, he'd meet with them, often one-on-one, to explain the rationale behind the decision. "These guys had really been the lead pilots, the technical pilots, who got us into the fleet type," he recalled. "They just poured themselves into establishing Horizon as a leading operator of this airplane, and now our decision to get out of it was just like a kick in the groin. They took it personally."

In addition, these pilots were smart and assertive opinion leaders within the company, and they didn't think the move made any business sense. They'd offer up reasonable but passionate arguments—prudently, from a management perspective—for keeping the planes. And Pinneo would hear them out in individual meetings. "It was worth however long it took to spend time with them, to hear them, to make sure I wasn't missing anything, and to walk them through the logic on why this is the most appropriate direction for the airline as a whole to take over time and to recognize the impact on them personally. It's not just about flying a different airplane; as I said, it's their baby."

By taking that time, Pinneo built a deeper level of respect with these pilots, even if they never did agree with the decision. When he thinks about one pilot in particular, a superstar within the pilot ranks we'll call Chuck, he remembers in great detail how the conversation transpired and how difficult it was. Chuck was seriously upset about the news. He'd done his homework, carefully outlined his argument, and was not about to accept the decision without firing his best shot at his boss.

Of course, Pinneo could have tasked another corporate leader to meet with Chuck, and I imagine his selfish ego whispering into his ear, *Delegate this one, Jeff. Delegate.* When asked about why he met with Chuck himself, Pinneo didn't hesitate. "Because it mattered to him," he said. "It mattered that I met with him. And as I think about it, during my whole experience and career at Horizon, I employed that rule of thumb: If it mattered to somebody else, that put it on the map, on the radar big time."

The one-on-one meetings between the CEO and each senior pilot didn't matter *only* to, say, Chuck. This manifestation of the culture Fusion Leadership creates didn't end when the conversation ended. It didn't occur in isolation. It gets to what I've mentioned in other chapters. That is, the ramifications of the meetings radiated outward, reverberating throughout the organization. "I'm sure the meetings had an impact on others who hadn't directly participated in them," Pinneo said. "I always presumed that a guy like Chuck would go away from those conversations and talk to others about it. In the worst cases, he'd say, 'I think Pinneo's lost his mind. I made my most compelling argument. He didn't get it. He didn't buy it. He's still on this track with this decision, and I don't agree with it.' But, at the same time, he would acknowledge to others that I made the time and showed the respect to listen to him. He'd probably say, 'But we talked about it face-to-face.'"

A Tale of Two Closings

While Pinneo was reconfiguring the business model at Horizon, the results of which led to that 2007 airlines award, he realized the carrier had to scale back. Consequently, he and his team decided to cancel service to a few cities and close a couple of flight crew bases. Clearly, this meant another round of delivering bad news, as the moves disrupted many people's lives, forcing them to travel more and spend more time and effort to do their jobs. In many cases, it undercut their seniority status. Pinneo talked about two different bases and two different approaches to announcing their closures— one done poorly, the other done as well as could be expected. The contrast between the two offers a case study in corporate communication and Fusion Leadership.

The first base closure occurred in a small city in the western United States that Pinneo doesn't want identified. "For anyone involved who reads this, it would just reopen old wounds," he said. In announcing this closure, Pinneo, who was then a vice president of Horizon, urged his boss, the CEO (who will also remain nameless) to go to the base, hold a meeting of some 150 employees, announce the news, and answer questions. "He really didn't want to deliver the news himself, but a few of us thought that he should, that the CEO needed to be there," he said. As I listened to Pinneo tell the story, I wondered if that CEO struggled, at that time, with his own selfish-ego temptations, seeking to avoid the travel and the heartache and yearning to delegate the job.

Pinneo and some others in upper management accompanied the CEO, who would prepare for the meeting on the flight from Seattle to the other city. But while they were all waiting at the gate to depart from Seattle, a disgruntled Horizon pilot came over to the CEO and started ranting to him about a change in his hotel assignment that had really upset him. "He was really ragging on [the CEO]," Pinneo recalled, adding that his boss got very upset about the encounter and, during the entire flight, was "steaming" about what a big deal the pilot had made out of a trivial nonissue. "The point is he went into the meeting with that frame of mind, and it went very badly."

During the meeting, employees grilled the CEO, and one person in particular really got under the executive's skin, making him lose his temper. "This one guy, one of the captains, is a master at moving your needle," Pinneo said. "I mean, he's incredibly crafty and articulate, and he can slice you and dice you with words, and you don't even know how it's happened. But I absolutely learned a ton. That was an indelible moment for everyone in the room, and I think, more than anything, I learned that if you lose your temper, you're gone. You're done. There's just no way to recover. [The experience] affected my strategies for everything after that—especially when I became CEO. I probably had two or three times where I flew to [that city] just to see [the slice-and-dice captain], to meet him on his turf for a coffee or something like that, because, first of all, he's wicked smart. I was just fascinated by his intellect and the way he thought about things, and he's clearly an opinion leader. So part of my strategy was to try to seek out the detractors and see if I could build a dialogue with them because I knew people were listening to them."

Now let's look at the second closure, in Spokane, Washington, which went as smoothly as possible. In that situation, the leadership team didn't fly in and surprise the employees there with the bad news. Management announced the closure *before* Pinneo and some other vice presidents—no CEO this time—visited the base for a meeting; that is, they didn't spring the news on them. And the announcement included an information packet with frequently asked questions and answers about the decision and its effects on Horizon, its employees, and its customers.

"It was much more like an open-house format than a meeting to drop a bomb on them," he said, in reference to the previous closure announcement. "I think, for a lot of reasons, it just went better that way, because the news was out, and people had had time to go through a few of the phases of shock, denial, grief, and acceptance. People wanted to know *What does it mean for me?* And we were prepared on that level. In fact, we even had a few of the schedulers and others who could actually run scenarios. So there was more of a workout component to it."

In Spokane, Pinneo and his colleagues did a much better job of valuing the dignity of their people than they did in the other city.

"It helped that it was more informal in Spokane and that people were coming and going," he said, adding that the decision to establish the "open-house" environment demonstrates the importance of learning from your mistakes.

Donating Time and Health

The Spokane experience also shows how a culture that treats everyone with respect can ease workplace tension, make a bad situation bearable, and help an organization reach success in the long run. Under Pinneo's leadership, Horizon became well regarded as a leader in the industry, with a very desirable work environment. That's something Pinneo talks about—when asked, that is; he's too humble to gloat about that and often gives credit to others, like Horizon founder Milt Kuolt and Bill Ayer, who was the CEO of Alaska Airlines and one of Pinneo's mentors. "I think Horizon's reputation was and is a very good one, as a first-class operator, a highly sophisticated, technically oriented, well-respected airline among the technical groups, the pilots, mechanics, and others," he said. "And it's known throughout the industry as a great place to work."

One reason why people have been drawn to Horizon is that its employees are encouraged to care about each other and consider themselves members of a team—or even a family. For instance, employees asked for and received a change in company policy that allowed them to donate some of their vacation time to their colleagues if, for example, someone was battling cancer and needed more time off for treatment. Management, however, did place a limit on how much a person could donate. "We wanted to affirm the importance of [the donors] taking care of themselves, too," Pinneo said. "It made a statement: You matter too."

But employees sometimes give more than vacation days to their colleagues, and when talking about this, Pinneo expanded the definition of the company's culture. "We were a culture of giving," he said. "One employee donated a kidney to another. I mean, that just blew my mind. It was an employee, if I remember right, in another city. They weren't even coworkers. It was amazing."

I've never heard of that before—within a family, sure, but within a company, for someone to donate a kidney? That's remarkable. It's also a testament to the workforce and work environment that Jeff Pinneo helped create, which make the company different from its competition. "For us, the huge differentiator was—and is—people and the culture," he said. "A culture of mutual respect is the hardest to replicate. It's precious when you have it. It destroys you if you don't have it."

DIFFICULT FUSION LEADERSHIP: DOING THE DIRTY WORK AS CLEANLY AS POSSIBLE

On a cold, crisp winter day in early 2002, with bright Denver sunshine streaming through the windows of a large conference room, I stood and spoke before more than sixty people I'd gathered together. As I talked and scanned the crowd, one woman in the front row caught my attention. She was looking at me with penetrating blue eyes, crying quietly, and listening intently. And, through no fault of her own, she flustered me. I addressed everyone in the room, but I couldn't help but fixate on those misty blue eyes, feeling a nearly overwhelming sense of worry and responsibility.

That day, I did something I'd never done before—and it was dreadful.

But before I get too far into recounting that horrible experience, I'd like to share some thoughts about one of the leadership techniques Jeff Pinneo used. In the previous pages, I wrote about his encounter with Charlie Bucks, a vice-president of Continental Airlines, early in Pinneo's career, when he was a flight attendant. You'll recall that when this powerful and popular airline executive boarded the flight to Houston, he greeted Jeff by name and shook his hand. That thoughtful gesture—and the trouble and time Bucks took to know and use the name of the young employee he'd never met—resonated deeply with Pinneo. Later, as CEO of Horizon Air, he made it a practice to learn about his employees and use their names. He understood that this investment of time and energy helped create a work environment in which respect is reciprocal.

When I heard about this practice, it brought to mind an approach we employed at Integra Telecom. My great friend and fellow Integra Telecom leader Jim Huesgen, who served as our president for several years, came up with a brilliant exercise that we used regularly in the mid-2000s. That was a period of steady growth for the company, and we were constantly hiring people.

Every week, we had new-employee training classes at many locations. Jim or I would join the class in Portland for an hour or two each session, and we'd often both sit around the table with the new employees, introduce ourselves, and talk about the strategy of the company and what made us different in the marketplace. And here's the technique that Jim brought to the table: Before going into these classes, we'd study the photos and resumes of the five to ten new employees to memorize their faces, their names, and the personal information they had provided to our human resources team—things like where they attended college, what they liked to do on vacation, their favorite music, hobbies, and other interests.

The employees were expecting the traditional introduction with an exchange of names, handshakes, and small-talk pleasantries: "Some weather we've been having . . . blah-blah-blah." Instead, Jim and I broke any pattern of predictability. We'd address each person and use her name before she got the chance to introduce herself—and the new employees wouldn't be wearing name tags: "Hello, Mary. I'm really glad to get to meet you. I understand you went to college in Arizona and like to go backpacking in the mountains. I do a bit of that myself." I'd add the last line to show we had something in common but only, of course, if it were true. And then I'd quickly bring the conversation back to Mary and her background. I tell you, it would astound these people that the president or the CEO would take the time to know who they were and something personal about them.

Making a Mark that Lasts

I think this experience was powerful, and I know it left a lasting impression. To this day, people contact me who work or have worked at Integra Telecom and remember these introductions. One guy in particular, Eric, who's in Portland and became one of that market's top sales reps, still refers to the very first time we met during the two-day training and what he thought of the introductions. A few times over the years, he's told me, "I can't believe you took the time to learn about my life and talk about my interests and background during that training session." He loved this first encounter and made it clear that he immediately felt a genuine sense of connection with me and, by extension, the company.

So it really resonated with me when, years later, I heard the impact Charlie Bucks had on Jeff Pinneo when he got on the plane and demonstrated that he knew who the young flight attendant was and used his name. Isn't it intriguing that, in a completely different setting, in a completely different industry, the same approach carried an equally profound impact?

What really interests me about the technique we used at Integra Telecom training sessions is that Jim, the president, was the champion of the idea. This underscores the notion that, when Fusion Leadership is thriving and the roots are penetrating deeper into the soil of the organization and the trunk is growing stronger and broader, other people start adopting the tools and the power of the collective ego. This was Jim's idea, his initiative, and he deserves all the credit for it. I'm not for a moment suggesting that I did anything to bring it out of him. He would have brought it out anyway, because he's just that kind of person. And he did—interestingly, some four or five years after he came to Integra Telecom.

But I will say that when this notion of reciprocal respect takes root in an organization and its members become motivated to perpetuate the power of this leadership tool, people bring forward innovation and inspiration. And not just the CEO. As I've mentioned, a work environment with this kind of atmosphere produces ideas and outcomes from all kinds of people in a positively infectious manner. It triggers a chain reaction of creativity and accomplishment.

What's more, we enhance the broader strength of this phenomenon by pushing aside that pesky, narcissistic, selfish ego. For example, while I usually looked forward to these around-the-table introductions, I must admit that, sometimes, I didn't want to take the half an hour or so required to memorize the names, photos, and information of the new employees, like I was cramming for a final exam at college. My selfish ego would rather linger longer at lunch or even over-prepare for the upcoming board meeting so that I could impress that constituency. But I knew I'd benefit from the feverish studying I'd do. So I sublimated Mr. Selfish Ego and made the time and energy investment, and Jim did too. Consequently, we reaped enormous satisfaction from the introduction sessions and would come away from them energized. More importantly, the company benefited from this potent leadership tool. But then again, one of the themes of this model of leadership is *When your organization benefits, you benefit*. Embrace that.

These introductions also served as a bonding mechanism among the employees of that incoming class of new hires. The conversation would reveal, for example, that Charlotte's hobby is gourmet cooking, and Michael would pipe in, "I like to think I know my way around the kitchen pretty well too, especially when it comes to French cuisine." These two foodies might later talk about their common interest or even share recipes. And this sense of collegiality would emerge without any forced "team-building games" that usually get most people rolling their eyes and checking out mentally. Who cares what type of workplace animal you are and what you can do to get along with the other animals in the jungle? True collegiality and collaboration reveal themselves naturally.

The word *naturally* is the key here. That is, let me issue a word of warning. With this approach, you absolutely must show genuine interest in your new employees. If you have to fake it, don't use this tool, because they'll see right through you, and the relationships with them will start off under a thick cloud of phoniness. You can't come across as a snake oil salesman trying to manipulate the new hires' impression of the organization. Your efforts have to come from a place of sincere respect.

Another thing—draw a line when discussing personal lives, and don't cross it. You need to steer wide and clear of compromising somebody's privacy. You're really just welcoming people to the company and letting them know that you care about their lives outside of the workplace. By doing so, you're also sending an important message: The company values each person who works here. We're going to take our time to invest in you. And we expect this will enhance our culture and that you're going to buy into our strategy and mission and do great things for our customers. Just as we invest in you, we expect you to invest in our customers.

I can say with certainty that this approach worked for us.

Recession Blues: Something's Got to Give

Okay, now about that crowd of people I was addressing in the Integra Telecom facility at the Denver Tech Center in 2002. At that time, of course, the nation was stuck in the middle of the dot-com recession. The Dow Jones had dropped by more than 50 percent and the NASDAQ by more than 70 percent. Capital was simply not available; the capital markets had effectively closed. Everywhere you looked, companies were downsizing their workforces.

This was a time when Integra Telecom was at the very beginning of its growth curve. We were burning through cash and not yet cash-profitable. Companies in our industry were closed out of the market, so we couldn't raise more money. Businesses were going bankrupt all around us. It became very clear to me that the only way our company would survive was if we got by on the remaining amount of cash we had, which would be difficult, as we were ripping through millions of dollars a month, and our expenses exceeded our revenues.

We had just launched our Colorado operations a year before. The cost of expanding into a new state was about $500,000 a month. Typically, it took fifteen to twenty months for that state to become self-sufficient. So a half-million dollars a month times fifteen to twenty months was—well—you can do the math. It's a lot of money. I did the math, and I thought about the five markets we had at the time: *Oh my gosh, we've expanded from Oregon to four additional markets, so we're attempting to build five in total, and we might very well run out of money.* And, as I looked at the world around us, I knew that would be the equivalent of flying the plane into the side of the mountain.

After very difficult deliberations with the Integra Telecom board, I concluded that we had to close down one of the markets. We thought a lot about which one to shutter, and Colorado came to the top of that analysis, because it had opened quite recently, which meant it needed a longer time frame to become profitable. It would eat more cash in what was an especially competitive market, and it faced several challenges.

So I made the difficult, gut-wrenching decision to close Colorado.

And that explains the tears coming from those intense blue eyes. This woman and every one of the other sixty or so Rocky Mountain–based Integra Telecom employees were learning that they were losing their jobs.

One of the things that I should emphasize about any leadership style, and it's certainly true in the Fusion Leadership approach, is that people should not confuse advancing the organization and investing in the collective ego as being any form of democracy. As the CEO, I owned the responsibility. It had been my strategy to execute; it was my job to make the tough calls. I felt I had a duty to the entire organization to take whatever steps were necessary to secure our future and ensure our success. Therefore, I made the call to close down this market. It was emotionally horrible, and I agonized.

At that point in my career, five years after I started the company, I was relatively inexperienced as a leader, and honestly, I had probably only fired two or three people in my entire life. All I knew about firing employees was that I hated the task. It's the most awful thing to have to do because you know that their lives are forever changed. You hope they bounce back, but even if they do, you know that you're sending them into a period of turmoil in their lives. You realize that most of these people have mortgages to pay and families to feed. Having to fire staff is the most heartbreaking thing I've had to do in my entire career.

In the days before I announced my decision, I thought about the act of pink-slipping more than sixty people and found myself overwhelmed with anxiety about how I would do that. I'd never before thought through the logistics of pulling off something like that. This was a big event in the company's life and for me personally. I decided to go to Colorado with our vice president of human resources, Lisa Hillyer. We laid out a plan. Unlike Jeff Pinneo, who announced the closure of the Spokane base before he arrived and then showed up to conduct an open house where people could ask questions, I made the decision to fly in and drop the bomb. I was going to pull everyone together in the room and tell them all at once, in person. But thanks to my collaboration with Lisa, we did have a strategy going into it.

The day before we convened the Colorado employees, we met with the vice presidents. In that market, there were four vice presidents, including the general manager. We told them that we were there to do something very horrible: "Not only are the four of you getting terminated, we're going to close down the entire market." That meeting ended up being a smart thing to do, because we had a lot of work ahead of us. We had many customers, and you can't just cut them off. They had entrusted their data services to us. We couldn't just unplug our business, drop their communications on the floor, and walk out of the state. We had to have a skeletal team of people stay on for six months who would help these customers migrate to other companies, our former competitors in Colorado. We had to work with the landlord to clean up the building. We had to sell our furniture. It was a lot to manage.

To a large extent, I devised my game plan on the fly—literally, as Lisa and I discussed strategy on our flight from Portland to Denver. It was nowhere near as well thought out as what Jeff did in Spokane. But the meeting with the vice presidents was good, because it allowed me to refine my thoughts and finalize the plans with their input. It also gave me the opportunity to check in with each one of them to make sure, before they went home that night, that they had enough emotional stability to be able to handle the fallout from the next day's meeting with the employees and all the work that had to be done.

Dropping the Bomb, Losing Composure

That next morning, as the employees were filling the room and mingling, I looked out over the crowd, thinking, *These people have no idea what I'm about to tell them.* That just made me more nervous. Now, I could have delegated this dirty deed, but I felt that it was my job to deliver the bad news, much like how Pinneo met in person with the pilots to tell them about the decision to ground their favorite fleet of airplanes. As I saw these people milling about, in good spirits on a bright sunny day, I thought, *I'd rather be almost anywhere else in the world than at this place, at this time, with this job I have to do.*

I started the meeting, briefly commended the employees' hard work and accomplishments, and then got right to the point. "We're in this horrible recession," I said. "As you know, we've raised a lot of capital, but we won't be able to raise any more capital in this economic environment. The most important thing to me is to ensure the survival of our company, and, because you're our newest market and because of other considerations, I made the decision to shut the Colorado operations down."

As I spoke, I became overwhelmed by a thought I couldn't let go of: *What did these people do to deserve this?* These were educated, hard-working people. Part of what got them here was that they became energized around a vision I had articulated. I told them we were going to have this fresh new competitive model about investing in the customer and providing this wonderful customer service model locally. These were people who used to work at AT&T, Qwest, and other well-established telecom companies. They took the risk and rallied behind my vision, and, because they did, they had to hear me tell them they were out of work. I felt an enormous weight of responsibility and couldn't shake the feeling that I had somehow let these people down.

While all this rattled around in my mind, I kept on delivering the message, telling them what needed to get done to migrate our customers. I described their generous severance package and that I made it a priority to ensure that people were not left out in the cold without any bridge to another job. I would often get criticized by my board for providing what they thought was an overly generous severance package. I did that because everyone in the other four markets that survived would look at this and say, *How would Integra Telecom treat me if they closed down my market?* I wanted to send a message that we treated people well so the remaining employees didn't start looking for jobs because they were worried about the rug being pulled out from under them.

And I kept returning my focus to the woman crying in the front row, thinking about how this was going to affect her. I wondered if she had a family and if she had bills that had piled up for some reason. Was she crying because she was afraid of some circumstance I couldn't appreciate? Was she crying just because it was a very emotional time in the room? I was transfixed by her. I ended up breaking down and getting misty-eyed and stuttering a little in my delivery of the message. I allowed myself to become too emotional. That was a time when those people needed their leader to be strong and stoic. You don't want to be gleeful, of course, but you also don't want to convey weakness at that time.

Here's the takeaway: This notion of the collective ego and that you invest yourself in other people and create this culture of mutual respect—there's a line you need to be careful not to cross. You can't get overly attached. You need to be a little dispassionate.

I was doing my job by protecting the larger company and firing these people. It would've been fine for me to stand on that principle. But I became too empathetic, which enabled the whole group to become more emotional. As the meeting wound down, it felt like we were at a funeral. Everyone was walking around with their heads down. Many were crying. It didn't have to go that far. I shouldn't have fixated on the woman with blue eyes, but I couldn't help it. She was right in front, and her eyes were so piercing that I couldn't look away from her.

In that situation, it's the leader's role to set the right tone and pull things together in a way that lets people move ahead with their lives. After my brief lapse, I did just that.

Lisa was great and had a lot more experience than I did in dealing with these things. She handed out documents with answers to frequently asked questions, elaborated on our very good severance plan, explained that the health benefits would carry through for several weeks, talked about the outplacement training we would provide, and told the employees that they could use the office for a couple of weeks to get their resumes together. We tried to be as helpful as possible.

I stuck around one more day after delivering the bad news to make sure the VPs were going to be able to close the office as smoothly as possible. I got my own emotional act together and was able to walk the floor and help answer questions directly. Some people asked if I would write letters of recommendation or if I could make introductions with other companies in town, and, of course, I obliged to the best of my ability. Lisa and I were able to help them move forward.

The Right Move

The question arises: Did I make the right call in shutting down our Colorado operations? The answer is a definitive yes. Following that closure, we became cash-flow positive by the end of 2002. It allowed the other four markets to push on and become the backbone of a company that ultimately served eleven states and employed thousands of people.

In fact, we ended up getting back into Colorado five years later, through an acquisition, and were able to hire back some of the people we had to terminate in 2002. Many rejoined the company without any hard feelings, because we'd renewed our investment in them.

More about What's in a Name

Before ending this chapter, I want to revisit the importance of names. You'll recall Jeff Pinneo's practice of walking down an airport concourse and greeting all of the Horizon employees by name. That matters to people. I used to do something similar all the time, and it helped foster the type of work environment we wanted at Integra Telecom.

Most of our twenty-two different offices housed expensive network equipment, requiring security guards and swiping a company-issued electronic ID badge to gain entry. The security guards were not Integra Telecom employees, because we contracted with security companies for the service. I used to make a point of knowing the names of those guards. Jim did this as well.

Furthermore, any time I was in front of a group of employees talking about the results for that month or the budget for the year or sharing the priorities of the company, I would always make a point somewhere in my presentation to weave in the name of that particular office's security guard or receptionist. For example, Igor was the name of the guard at our Portland office, and I remember mentioning him in an office-wide talk about the goals for that year.

It would go something like this: "Just today, as I was walking in and greeting Igor, he made a comment about some clutter that had been sitting in a corner of the room. He took it upon himself to clean it up so the presentation of the company would be that much better. And that investment on his part is a good way to think about these goals for the year."

I think most employees would go to work and walk right by the front-door person. It wouldn't occur to them to invest a moment of their time to get to know his or her name or anything about him or her. This is not to say that the employees didn't like meeting new people. It's just that they were busy and had things on their mind.

My theory was that, by making that brief mention of Igor, people would walk out of that meeting feeling that I challenged them to greet and get to know the security guard or the person at the front desk better. I hoped that would be enough of a challenge that they might then apply this same behavior in dealing with the company's customers and other employees in the organization.

Using names is also another way of communicating the value of each person, which helps create the best possible work culture. Indeed, this sense of cohesiveness is precious when you have it. It destroys you if you don't have it. And it helped guide me when it came to delivering bad news.

CHAPTER 4

WHO OWNS THE CRISIS?

COMMUNICATE, COLLABORATE, AND CONTRIBUTE: FUSION LEADERSHIP IN THE AFTERMATH OF WAR AND NATURAL DISASTER

In early spring 1991, several United States Army officers met with their chaplain in the desert in Saudi Arabia, not far from the Saudi–Iraqi border. US forces had just conducted Operation Desert Storm about as fast and effectively—from a military perspective—as was possible, defeating Saddam Hussein and driving his troops from their temporary occupation of Kuwait. The Persian Gulf War was over, famously, in one hundred hours.

But the work was far from done. And, like many of their fellow soldiers, this group of leaders continued to depend on the inspirational counsel of their chaplain, Tommy Creston. They had a tall task ahead of them: to wash and scrub hundreds of bulldozers, scrapers, bucket loaders, tractor-trailers, and other vehicles so they could be shipped out of the post–war zone. That meant a massive cleaning job of all the equipment for the whole division, which comprised 50,000 people. Seven wash racks were built on the hard-packed sand, all of which were open twenty-four hours a day. Each unit had a prescribed period of time to use these racks based on the number of pieces of equipment it had.

"Some of us called it *the Battle Against the Department of Agriculture of the Nation of Saudi Arabia*, because we had to get our equipment clean enough to clear Saudi customs and bring it all back," General Robert Van Antwerp told me. At the time, he was an Army lieutenant colonel and the commander of the 326th Engineer Battalion, 101st Airborne Division, in charge of more than four hundred people (and as many as 650 people earlier in the conflict).

It was an enormously challenging, high-pressure job, with a big time crunch. Van Antwerp's soldiers waited in line with many other troops in the hot, dusty, eighty-plus-degree days and the chilly, forty-degree desert nights as they prepared to take their twenty-four-hours-a-day, seven-day shift scouring caked-on sand and mud off heavy, expensive, motorized implements of war. Van Antwerp and his commanding officers needed to devise an efficient plan for their men and women to perform this daunting mission, within deadline, so they could get back home to their family and friends. They came up with a solid strategic plan and were nearly ready to put it into action.

But before they did, Van Antwerp and many of his fellow leaders sought guidance from the chaplain. During one of Chaplain Creston's services, he offered his small congregation a gentle—and, as it turns out, prescient—piece of advice that deeply moved and motivated Van Antwerp, who vividly remembers the chaplain's words: "The chaplain said, 'You need to look for opportunities to wash your soldiers' feet. I don't know what that's going to look like, but, if you start seeking it out, you're going to get an opportunity to do it.' When he said that, I started looking for ways I could serve the people."

It wouldn't take long before such an opportunity to serve his soldiers raised its head and looked Van Antwerp straight in the eye, resulting in an experience that shaped his approach to leadership for the rest of his life.

Leadership Philosophy: "The Big Four"

I'll get to that career-altering event in a little while, but first, it's important to understand more about this man, who I'm fortunate to have as a friend. Van, as he's called by some of his civilian friends, and General Van to many in the military, grew up in a large family led by a strong role model. "I came from a big family, and we always had a service component," he said. "My father started his own business, and I learned about service, leadership, and hard work from him."

During his school years, Van Antwerp played team sports, and his coaches and teammates almost always selected him to be the captain; he was a natural leader at an early age. After high school, he attended and graduated from the United States Military Academy and went on to earn a master of engineering degree in mechanical engineering from the University of Michigan and, later, an MBA from Long Island University. But, first and foremost, he was a soldier and an officer in the US Army, serving in many different capacities over his thirty-nine-year military career, which culminated with a promotion to three-star general as chief engineer of the US Army and an appointment as the chief of the Army Corps of Engineers in 2007. Currently a retired general, he serves on the corporate boards of five companies.

Over the years and in his various leadership roles, Van Antwerp has learned a lot about what it takes to guide others and successfully take on seemingly impossible projects. As Army Corps chief, he oversaw 37,000 people, directing many of them in the massive recovery efforts to rebuild and protect New Orleans after Hurricane Katrina devastated the Crescent City and its surrounding areas (more on this case study in crisis management later).

Along the way, he's developed a guiding philosophy, with four distinct planks, from which he draws in times of need. I think these principles fall in line with the Fusion Leadership model I've come to embrace. "I often talk about the Big Four," he said. "One: The leader has to create a vision. You have to know where you're going. Two: You have to influence others to go with you. There are going to be some doubters and people who don't have their hearts in it in the first place. But you have to persevere and lead them. Three: You have to serve. Four: You have to develop people. Part of developing leaders is to get them the right experience. I think that experience in the desert after Desert Storm was a great event for service, and it was an incredibly great event for developing the subordinate leaders."

So exactly what did happen during the hot days and cool nights in Saudi Arabia that carried such an impact on Van Antwerp? Well, it was an important and unusual decision he made and critical follow-through action he performed, which embodies an intrinsic component of Fusion Leadership.

Rolling Up the Sleeves

At about six in the evening on the fourth day of the weeklong washing shift, Van Antwerp and the second-in-command leader ventured over to the wash rack to inspect their soldiers' progress. What they saw startled them. They encountered exhaustion incarnate. "We found people lying down underneath a bucket loader, sleeping in the mud," Van Antwerp said, adding that one soldier lay dead asleep with a washing wand still in his hand. "We knew right then that we had a huge dilemma. We had devised what we thought was a great plan: We knew how many people we needed at each wash station, how long they'd work, when we were going to get a vehicle on the rack, and how long it would take to wash each vehicle—but we didn't expect or plan for the fatigue factor."

Put another way, Van Antwerp said, he didn't figure the human dimension into the scheme of things. Today, he jokes about that important element in all leadership decisions and plans of action. "Something I say today is this: Leadership would be great if it didn't involve people," he said with a chuckle.

But anyway, Van Antwerp and his fellow leader looked at the situation, knowing that the consequences of not finishing in seven days were enormous. He and his troops could start their journey home—away from the desolate desert sand and onto welcoming US soil, where they'd be greeted by family and friends—if only they could finish washing all the vehicles assigned to them within their seven-day shift. And they couldn't take an extra day or even an extra hour. "Out of respect and fairness, you had to get out of the way of the next unit coming in, so that's why we only had seven days," Van Antwerp said. "If you didn't get done in time, you had to go to the end of the line." And that would significantly delay their return trip home.

So, as the chill of the desert evening air descended on them and with their dog-tired troops asleep or halfway there, the two leaders pondered their dire circumstances. Finally, the officer turned to his leader, Van Antwerp, and offered his assessment. "The sergeant major said to me, 'You know, we have a lot of people who haven't washed a single vehicle,'" Van Antwerp recalled.

"I immediately thought about myself, but I said, 'Name a couple of people who haven't done it.' He said, 'You. And me. And the company commanders. And the senior noncommissioned officers.' And he continued going down the line of command until I interrupted him and said, 'I got it. I got it.'"

Van Antwerp immediately figured out how many of his team's leaders they needed. Within two or three hours, they had rounded up enough people so that he, his sergeant major, and a few dozen subordinate commanders could relieve their exhausted soldiers and begin a twenty-four-hour shift down in the cold, wet mud, with scrub brushes and washing wands in hand and the sounds of heavy-duty generators serenading them through the night and into the next day.

But before the commanders could excuse the people they were replacing, they needed instruction—in what turned out to be an intriguing case of role reversal, with the soldiers leading the leaders. "That was very interesting, because you had a bucket loader operator telling the battalion commander what to do, how to clean the vehicle," Van Antwerp said. "We went into our shift not knowing what we were doing at all. We went into it knowing that they were the experts. They taught us."

That is, after the initial shock wore off, because the soldiers' first reaction was one of incredulity. "It was pretty funny," Van Antwerp recalled, "because they were saying things like, 'Sir, so you're really going to do this?' and they were smiling and chuckling. But they were very gracious about it and instructed us on how to get the job done right. And of course, it was great news to them because they were so tired."

Now, back in the early nineties, before the rise and ubiquity of the Internet, word didn't travel as fast as it does today. But still, news of this development spread as quickly as a viral singing cat on a YouTube video does today. A head-over-heels flip had occurred at that wash rack there in the Saudi desert, with the supervisors working and the workers supervising. The commanders were figuratively washing the feet of the soldiers by literally washing the wheels of the vehicles. "The first thing I thought of when we decided to work the wash rack was, *Aha, this is what the chaplain meant,*" Van Antwerp said. When the chaplain came by and saw him and his battalion leaders doing the dirty work, he told Van Antwerp, "Well, at least one of my messages got through to somebody."

WHAT WOULD THE GENERAL THINK?

Naturally, I can't hear this story without considering the selfish-ego-versus-collective-ego tension at work here. I imagine that, somewhere in the general's brain, the selfish ego voice must have been whispering to him to reject the sergeant major's suggestion that the officers relieve the exhausted soldiers on the wash rack: *It's cold and muddy and requires a lot of hard physical labor. You're the highest-ranking officer in this battalion, and you've already paid your dues. You're above all of this. Let the foot soldiers do the grunt work. Besides, if you and the other officers do this, who will lead the troops?*

But of course the collective ego voice prevailed, and I imagine it saying something like this: *The men and women under your command need you to do the right thing. They want to go home—and so do you. It's in your best interests and, more importantly, the best interests of the battalion to grab a washing wand and start cleaning. You're the leader, so lead!*

I asked Van Antwerp about this, and he didn't really seem to experience much of a struggle; the selfish ego voice wasn't concerned about twenty-four hours of chilly, wet, demanding work. But he did hesitate, if only for an instant, as he thought about the reaction that the division commander, who was fondly known as

"General Benny P," would have when he learned about the officers doing this kind of work. While Van Antwerp didn't think he'd find himself in any trouble, he did wonder if the two-star general would "think this was really weird," he said. "Nowhere else he went did he see the officers of the battalion washing vehicles."

Well, in the middle of the night, several hours into their shift, Van Antwerp and his officers learned what the general thought about this. "At about two or three in the morning, when it was cold and we were wet and we were working, General Benny P and his command sergeant major were going around to the various wash racks to see how people were doing. By the way, that in and of itself is a wonderful example of what leaders do and how they use their time. He did the same thing during the war; he was at the point of attack; he was at the toughest part. And during the recovery phase and return-home phase of the operation, he was out there. He came down the line, and I could hear his voice before he got to my station. I knew who it was. My initial feeling returned: *What's he going to think? Would he consider it odd?* Well, he and I had a conversation and . . . he thought what we were doing was one of the greatest things he'd ever seen or heard."

COLLABORATING FOR SUCCESS

Over the next three and a half days, the officers and the soldiers toiled alongside each other, talking and sometimes laughing as they worked against each other in friendly competition. Simply put, the infusion of the extra help on the wash rack—especially considering who was providing that help—gave the battalion a huge morale boost. And, of course, it allowed the members of the battalion to spread out the workload and get much-needed rest. The experience also served as a bonding mechanism. "We were talking it up and making fun of the situation," Van Antwerp said with a smile. "When you have a leader who gets dirty like that, you have a commonality because you're sharing the work, and that means you can communicate on a different level."

Not only did the battalion members make their seven-day

deadline; they freed up the rack for the next unit with a few hours to spare. "We made our goal and got to go home on time," Van Antwerp said.

As I listened to the general talk about the Battle Against the Department of Agriculture of the Nation of Saudi Arabia, I couldn't help but think that something else motivated him to make the decision to put himself and his officers on the rack. Yes, they wanted to meet the deadline. But did he have a more far-reaching agenda beyond the seven-day mission to evacuate equipment and troops out of the desert? I asked him this question. His answer didn't disappoint.

Van Antwerp, who identifies himself as a servant leader and conveys an innate sense of how to fuse teams together, had been thinking for some time about his contributions to the Army. He considered what would become point four in his philosophical Big Four—develop people—and he knew he was in charge of a handful of key officers he could teach how to become better leaders.

"I already felt that I was on my way to becoming a servant leader," he said. "This experience solidified it. I think it did in the minds of a lot of my subordinate leaders as well. Many of them went on to become full colonels, commanding brigades in the Army and commanding districts in the Corps of Engineers."

I heard the sense of accomplishment in his voice when he recalled those three and a half days. "While we were doing this," he said, "we started to compete: 'How quickly can you get your vehicle done?' It was a game, but, of course, it was also real work and real life. And it showed my subordinate leaders that this whole leadership thing can be exciting and fun. I always try to identify the talent for leadership and model behavior for them."

Clearly, this collaborative effort in the Saudi desert demonstrates what a passionate and committed workforce—in this case, a US Army battalion—can accomplish through the application of Fusion Leadership. Van Antwerp put aside his worries that General Benny P would react poorly to his decision and acted to serve the best interests of his organization, the collective ego. And not only did the general praise him at the time; he didn't forget what Van Antwerp and his officers did.

Several months later, Van Antwerp was assigned a change in command. He was invited to a ceremony at Fort Campbell, Kentucky, hosted by General Benny P, who wished farewell to the exiting commander, Van Antwerp, and welcomed in the new one. A band played on the parade field and was accompanied by a lot of fanfare. The general spoke for fifteen minutes about each of the two commanders, and, when he addressed the outgoing officer, he didn't spend much of his speech on Van Antwerp's illustrious career. Instead, he spent the bulk of his talk on one event. You guessed it—that half a week near the Saudi–Iraqi border.

"The general said, 'I know Van Antwerp did well in the war,' and he kind of left it at that but then went on to talk about the wash rack," Van Antwerp recalled. "He ended his speech by saying, 'And that's what leadership is all about. We want to thank you for being a great leader in the battalion.' Later on, the general was in a position to vote me in as a general. And I imagine he spoke highly of me before the board voted."

Although Van Antwerp didn't fully realize it at the time, the decision and the follow-through to work on that wash rack constituted a defining moment in his career as a leader. He now recognizes its significance. "That experience helped shape how I approach leadership, how I think about things," he said.

Katrina Crisis: The Not-So-Big Easy

I included Van Antwerp's desert anecdote in the book for several reasons. First, it's a compelling and previously untold story of US history that I think deserves to be captured in print. Second, it serves as a revealing portrait of effective leadership. Third, like Colleen Abdoulah did in Denver and I did in Minneapolis, General Robert Van Antwerp understood that listening to, learning from, and sometimes working with frontline employees are important tools of Fusion Leadership.

There are at least two other reasons for the story's inclusion. While I've spoken of the enormous benefits any organization gains from having an internal evangelist, an advocate, singing your organization's praises and inspiring others, that person doesn't always have to be someone in your charge. In this case, Van Antwerp's superior officer, General Benny P, became his biggest booster. So if you're a midlevel manager, keep in mind that you may find your company's vice president or even CEO recognizing your Fusion Leadership actions and, consequently, promoting you and your team's mission.

Finally, those three and a half days illustrate that the tenets and tools in this leadership model transcend the corporate world. By sublimating your selfish ego and embracing the collective ego, you can move your organization forward—whether you work in the nonprofit sector, academia, the legal profession, the military, or many other arenas.

I want to share another story that Van Antwerp told me. As mentioned earlier, he served as the chief of the Army Corps of Engineers and spearheaded the effort in 2007 to rebuild and protect New Orleans after the city and region suffered the wrath of Hurricane Katrina. The recovery efforts epitomize the engineering, management, and humanitarian marvel that American ingenuity and perseverance can achieve. And the feat that Van Antwerp and the Corps pulled off in rebuilding that wonderful and unique cultural center of our country really deserves pages and pages of narrative to do it justice. For our purposes, though, I just want to touch on a few key leadership traits that Van Antwerp exhibited in New Orleans.

First, here's a little background. When Katrina hit in August 2005, Van Antwerp was serving as lieutenant general in the sessions command, where he conducted recruiting and basic training for the Army. The Corps of Engineers had gone into New Orleans shortly after the hurricane struck and had started rebuilding or had been making plans to reconstruct the city, its levee system, and much of its entire infrastructure. But by the spring of 2007, the Corps seemed stuck in a quagmire, inching along in its reconstruction efforts at building a rudimentary initial recovery system while the residents of the Crescent City—and much of the rest of the nation—wanted fast action. Under fire and steeped in criticism, the Corps's chief engineer stepped down, a year before his four-year assignment was over.

Eager to right the ship, the US government turned to Robert Van Antwerp.

Usually, the Corps doesn't take someone of Van Antwerp's rank, at the time, to run the organization—but he was different. "I was a seasoned, crusty, thick-skinned lieutenant general, and they said, 'We want you to come down here and do this,'" he recalled. "When I took over, it was an organization that was under pressure from everybody locally, the congressional delegation from Louisiana, Congress, and even the president, who had made a commitment to build what's called a *one-hundred-year risk reduction system* for the greater New Orleans area. So, first, we had to do a lot of restoring of the public trust, dealing with that criticism coming from all angles, some of which was founded, most of which was not."

Van Antwerp calls this job a "monster," because he needed to oversee the Corps as its members tore down the existing levees and made new ones, put up surge barriers, and rebuilt pumping stations, among many other reconstruction projects.

Here's where he needed to place himself and his team into fusion mode. "I had to focus myself, the leadership, the whole Army Corps on serving others, because there was a lot of *us-versus-them* [division] happening. If you walked the neighborhood down to New Orleans, you saw that many of the people were so angry that they would almost be at the point of spitting on you. So, no matter how much they blamed us and others, we were going to focus our efforts on making the situation better and serving the nation this way."

Of course, Van Antwerp understood that a lot of the New Orleans citizens were still homeless and in desperate need of assistance on a variety of fronts. They also wanted open lines of communication, so he conducted town hall meetings to talk to and, more importantly, listen to the people. "They needed compassion and understanding," he said. "So, in the town halls, I'd take an hour or two just to allow people to vent and tell their situation and tell their story. We tried to link those people up with others who could give them answers, give them help. People would see our Corps trucks and want to know what we were doing. We'd equip them with maps of what we were doing. I wanted to be open and let them know that this wasn't about us. This was about the nation. So how could we pull together?"

That surely wasn't easy, and a leader who acts to appease the selfish ego would surely send in one of his or her subordinates to face the wrath and pain of the people. But Van Antwerp knew it was in the best interests of the residents as well as the members of the Corps that the top-of-the-line leader show up to the public meetings and—well—demonstrate leadership.

Serving with Transparency and Honesty

In crisis management—and, two years after the hurricane, New Orleans was clearly still in crisis, as was the Corps—a Fusion Leader needs to establish that his or her organization is committed to honesty and transparency. Van Antwerp used high-tech tools to help him do that.

He and his team approached Google and talked with the managers there about getting satellite maps of the region. The Corps posted the maps on its website so people could log on and find their house. "They could actually see their roof and driveway and whatever," Van Antwerp said. "And then they could look at an inundation map. This way, if a storm happened today, they could see what their house, their driveway, their basement would look like. We equipped the people with intelligence."

The Corps set up workshops, with computer banks so that residents could get the instruction and technology they needed to become more informed. "They could see two things on Google Earth," Van Antwerp explained. "We gave them a view of what the area would look like when we finished. Then they could push a button to see what it would like today if they had another Hurricane Katrina. Some needed to rebuild their homes on stilts. It was a reality check. Later, we got praised for being transparent."

In some ways, it would have been easier to work without the peering eyes of the public, but it wouldn't have advanced the mission as effectively.

Another tool Van Antwerp used to manage this massive project seems simple on the surface: relationship building. But this is something that's often overlooked by leaders and other times intentionally ignored, because cultivating trusting relationships requires devoting time and energy. Van Antwerp understood this completely.

"I set about building deep relationships, what later became friendships, with the people of Louisiana," he said. "I know every parish president in Louisiana. I went fishing with those guys. I ate dinner with them. I went to crawfish boils. And everybody else between me and them did the same thing. Once you build these relationships, what follows is trust and understanding. When we first got to Louisiana, there was no understanding. People said, 'Fix this,' and 'Why isn't this done yet?' They had no idea that it was going to take about $1 million a mile and 220 miles of levees."

But after Van Antwerp reached out to the people, they came to understand the enormity of the mission and eventually embraced him and his Corps. An agency that was once despised by the people became respected. By the time he left the Corps after his four-year term in 2011, New Orleans was far along the road to recovery. The great city known as The Big Easy was healing much better than most had predicted.

In the next section, I share an experience I had in crisis management, albeit one not nearly as important or dramatic or far-reaching as what Van Antwerp faced in New Orleans. But then, that was truly a unique situation. Still, on some level and at one time or another, leaders encounter crises. The Fusion Leader will meet those challenges head on, with the success—sometimes even the survival—of the organization as priority number one. And the Fusion Leader knows, with absolute certainty, who owns the crisis.

HIT BY "A HARD DOWN": USING FUSION LEADERSHIP TOOLS TO NAVIGATE A CRISIS

By 2007, Integra Telecom's dedicated employees, my leadership team, and I had the business sailing along at a brisk clip. We were growing our customer base, expanding into new markets, generating impressive revenues, and, important to me as a Fusion Leader, trusting each other to collaborate and work hard to offer top-notch, reliable service to the thousands of customers who depended on us.

I remember coming to my office in Portland one morning in the best of moods, despite the gray, wet, and rainy early-winter weather. I felt satisfied with my life, family, coworkers, and career, as well as Integra Telecom's mission and vision. I was figuratively skipping and whistling into work.

After greeting several people in the hallways, I entered my office, reviewed my calendar, made a couple of quick phone calls, and then checked my email. Just as I was about to close my in-box, a message came in from Tom, our head of network engineering. Within seconds, my buoyant mood sank like a stone. The title of Tom's email read, *We are down.* He went on to describe a dire situation: a network outage. At a large hospital in the Pacific Northwest. With a very important urgent and critical care center. In a fairly big metropolitan area several miles from any other qualified emergency health facility.

This was big. This was bad.

Now, let me step back for minute and say that the stories General Van Antwerp recalled in the previous pages are a tough act to follow. The situation I found myself in at that moment doesn't compare to the quandary the general confronted in the hot and unforgiving Saudi desert, and it certainly doesn't approach the crisis he faced in the aftermath of Hurricane Katrina in New Orleans. But an outage to a major regional hospital clearly registered to me and my staff as a full-blown crisis—one as bad as any we'd ever encountered.

Some of our data-routing devices in one of our hub operating centers had failed. In spite of built-in redundancy and our best engineering efforts, the entire hub crashed. And when a hospital network goes down—and this is no exaggeration—people's lives are at stake. Doctors, nurses, and health technicians need their data network to communicate with medical experts both inside and outside the hospital, to send files and imaging that might be critical to their diagnoses, and to help save patients in emergency situations. They also need their fully functioning communications network so that loved ones and family members can interact with patients. And on top of all that, they need to run a business. So it's a very big deal when a network hub goes down.

When I first read Tom's message, I was terrified. I thought, *Oh my gosh. What's going on? Why did this happen? What can we do?* It even triggered an irrational question in my mind: *Why did we ever agree to have them as a customer?* I knew immediately that this really was a crisis.

And, to a large extent, I was helpless.

That is, I was a bit of a bystander, because this type of network failure is highly technical. It goes immediately into the hands of the engineers. You engage in a comprehensive diagnostic procedure, first identifying where the network failure occurred. Once you identify that, you then move into the problem-solving process of determining what you have to do to repair or replace that part of the network. You need to know how many customers might be affected. Do you have the spare parts? Do you have the engineering capability on site, or do you need to have people flown in? How long is all this going to take? It's a very complex and technical set of circumstances to navigate, and, frankly, the CEO is not going to be able to add very much. It's really in the hands of the technical experts—fortunately, we had hired very good ones. I felt extremely confident in their expertise.

They also were very forthcoming with me, not holding back any important information. In some hierarchically structured organizations, employees conceal bad news from the boss. Not Integra Telecom engineers. They told me what they knew. I'd like to think the Fusion Leadership model from which I'd been working—one that fosters a culture of shared ownership—helped create such open and honest give-and-take exchanges.

Of course, I could help in other, nontechnical ways—specifically on the communication front inside our company, with the hospital executives, and, potentially, with the outside community. Knowledge of this type of event spreads quickly in a place like Integra Telecom, because it involves customers. Within about fifteen minutes, many people inside the organization were involved. The situation became highly visible within the company, and the employees were looking at how we'd handle all aspects of the crash.

Communicating with Candor

After I got the news, I walked over to where our vice president of network engineering was located. By that time, his office had become a huddle room, and his senior engineers were there, deep into the technical process of diagnosing the nature of the outage. I got my briefing from him. Because, as I mentioned, there wasn't much I could do on the technology end of things, I immediately started communicating with senior executives at the hospital. I gave them our absolute assurances that, at that moment, our highest priority was to get their network back up and running. They told me they'd suffered a substantial outage—what we call a *hard down*—and were unable to collaborate with medical experts outside of the facility, and even within the hospital, communication was difficult because the very large building comprises multiple wings.

Then I met with our public relations team to start preparing them for this tricky side of the crisis. We had on retainer an outside PR firm that has expertise in crisis management. We waited before bringing them in, because we were still in the middle of the storm, so to speak, and didn't have all the facts to determine the ultimate impact of the outage. But we were certainly gathering information as fast as we could and relaying what we found to the hospital, providing as many facts to them as we could.

In a crisis like this, it's imperative that you communicate honestly and transparently—a principle that guided General Van Antwerp in New Orleans. Because, let's face it, a lack of honesty and transparency has caused the downfall of many leaders and organizations. Remember the saying that originated from Watergate: "It's not the crime; it's the cover-up"? Well, obviously, no one had committed a crime here, but the same warning applied. Dishonesty and concealment in a crisis can cripple any organization, forever severing both external and internal trust. We didn't want to fall victim to that, which is one reason we were extremely candid and open with the hospital operations managers. The other underlying reason, though, is that it was simply the right thing to do.

So how did the situation play out? Because of our engineering team's feverish work, we were able to get the hospital's network up and running within about five hours of the crash. And, thankfully, no one was harmed during the crisis.

But we were worried that our relationship with a valued and important customer might be damaged. So, after we restored the network, we had to restore their trust. We had a meeting with them within twenty-four hours of the outage. I knew I had to see them face-to-face, so, with other company leaders, I traveled to the hospital. The focus of the conversation was the network, and the person who led the conversation was our senior vice president of network engineering. While we were all concerned about our relationship, this was not a time to talk about it. We had to demonstrate that we deserved their renewed trust. This was the time to lay out the network map, show them the exact devices that failed, explain to them why our network failed, and give them an engineered solution that would prevent it from ever happening again. We had a very specific plan of action.

Integra Telecom was essentially the hospital's sole telecom provider at the time, and we offered what some might consider a surprising recommendation: Hire one of our competitors to partner with us. We told them we'd build them a second entrance facility so that there would be two different communication highways into their building. And we recommended that the second entrance be connected to one of our competing telecom companies (in addition to ourselves) so that the hospital would have not only route diversity, by virtue of the second entrance, but also carrier diversity. In the long run, that would constitute a loss of revenue for us, but at the risk of being redundant, I have to say it again because it's just that important: This was all about restoring trust. We needed to prove that we were committed to their best interests and willing to sacrifice some of our business in the spirit of ensuring this would never happen again.

To Meet or Delegate?

To a much greater extent than what I heard from General Van Antwerp, this crisis presented me with yet another battle between the selfish ego and the collective ego, a struggle inherent in the Fusion Leadership model. But it didn't materialize where you might think it would. It wasn't about giving a competitor business that could have been ours. The selfish ego wanted the customer to be happy, and the collective ego wanted the customer to be happy, so, in what's an unusual happenstance, the two egos saw eye-to-eye on this one: The customer would be happy knowing that carrier diversity would make their network—and, consequently, their operations—the most secure.

Instead, the internal ego skirmish manifested in that initial meeting we convened in the immediate wake of the crisis. Emotionally, and selfishly, it would've been easier for me to delegate that responsibility and send my chief operating officer with my senior engineer and VP of customer care to meet with the hospital executives and not go myself. You know, stay out of what could be a painfully awkward situation. It's a humbling experience to sit in front of a major customer with your hat in your hand and say, "We screwed up. We put lives at risk because of the failure on our watch. We are so sorry." I could've told the hospital people that the CEO needed to man the fort back at headquarters. I certainly had that option.

I tried to manage Integra Telecom with the philosophy that, in the business of operating a complex data network, you're going to have outages. No network is perfect. You're going to have technical failures. What's most important is how you respond to those failures so that your customers are getting the best experience available in the marketplace. With that objective in mind, it was obvious to me that I had to attend that meeting. They needed to see that this was so important to our company that the CEO dropped what he was doing and was there within twenty-four hours, sitting in front of them and participating in the process of looking at the maps and explaining what caused the technical breakdown.

At that point, however, it was all still just talk. We had to actually deliver our plan, build a second entrance, and make sure another telecom company partnered in. We also had to be in constant communication with the hospital managers. We therefore conducted a series of weekly meetings over the next couple of months until the network was completely reconfigured and rebuilt. At the meetings, we'd show them the maps and progress reports.

So lesson number one from all this is to communicate with transparency and honesty and, in these specific circumstances, to lead with engineers and not with relationship managers. The second thing that was really important in the situation—because transparency and honesty by themselves are not enough—is to understand fully that you could have a world-class network plan, but unless you instill a sense of caring about the customer, you won't win them back. General Van Antwerp appears to have embraced the same philosophy when he instructed the Corps to walk the streets, accept public jeers, and share maps of the new dike and levy system. You have to place yourselves in their shoes to imagine what it would be like to be a surgeon with a digital image of a patient that you want to send to a prestigious national research hospital, like Oregon Health & Science University in Portland, Oregon, or the Mayo Clinic in Rochester, Minnesota, for expert analysis. Or maybe you're in the middle of a difficult and delicate surgery, and you're trying to decide exactly where to make an incision, so you need the expertise of a specialist in another city. And all of a sudden, through no fault of your own, your ability to communicate with those experts goes down. What's more, in circumstances like these, you have to ask what it would be like if that person being operated on is someone you love.

As a Fusion Leader, I felt we needed to exhibit an enormous sense of compassion for the doctors, nurses, and patients in the hospital. And I had an experience with that same hospital from which I could draw. It's located in the same city where my grandparents lived, and the last time I had physically been in this hospital was the last time I saw my grandfather alive, several years before. I was fortunate enough to have a grandfather who lived well into his nineties, but he suffered from a stroke or two at the end of his life and died during a similar time of year, the early winter, with the skies gray and the rain falling. So it was easy for me to have empathy for those inside the hospital, because I felt a profound sense of obligation to them. After all, they had treated my grandfather so well during his final weeks, days, and hours.

As part of the trust restoration efforts—and, clearly, our relationship had been tarnished—we continued to have frequent meetings with hospital personnel long after we got the network ramped up, the alternative entry built, and the competing telecom network serving as a backup. Not only did we successfully mend the rip to our reputation, we enhanced it by responding so well in this crisis and used the hospital as a reference to get other health care customers, including many hospitals in the region, using our service-diversity approach, which was born out of the crisis.

It certainly helped that the media didn't get wind of the outage and that no competitors discovered what happened, through corporate espionage or other means. Rivals in the dog-eat-dog telecom market wouldn't have hesitated to seize on something like this and use it to inflict damage to our reputation and pry away customers. But, luckily, we escaped virtually unscathed.

More than that, we flipped the crisis on its head by turning a dramatic and potentially company-destroying event to our long-term advantage. That is, we expanded our share of the health care market.

What Crisis? We Want To Celebrate

Communicating with transparency, driving credibility, and nurturing trust defuse a crisis most effectively and help build the fusion process. The Fusion Leader assigns equal importance to celebrating the wins with the same degree of transparency, credibility, and commitment to trust. That means directing credit to the people who earned it, whoever they are. That means body-slamming another executive who attempts to take the accolades for himself or herself at the expense of the employees who did the hard work. That means aligning your compensation system to reward the behaviors that generate the wins. That means taking time to celebrate wins often and with enthusiasm. That means many things, and it would be great fun to mine the community of successful leaders out there who have so effectively demonstrated these key tools that are equally vital to fusing an organization together.

At the risk of being negative, however, I chose to focus on the crisis side of the transparency, credibility, and trust spectrum, because I found that crises were tougher. They usually occur when least expected and can place an organization on an emotional high wire very quickly. On my journey, and with most leaders I know, it was always easier to lead when things were going well, rather than taking ownership and sharing the responsibility when confronted with a crisis.

A Credibility Challenge, a Gut Check

A couple of years after that transformative network outage occurred, during the depths of the Great Recession, in 2009, another potential crisis popped up, stared me in the face, and threatened my leadership credibility. And the person creating this threat—who I'll call Bill—was a friend of mine who I knew well. At least, I thought I knew him well.

Bill was a very successful midlevel leader in Seattle and a top-performing revenue generator; as they say in the legal profession, he was a rainmaker. I always knew I could count on Bill to get the job done and get it done well. When he and I were in the same office complex, we would sit and talk about business, travel, family, hobbies—you name it. He's an outgoing and likeable guy, but, as it turns out, maybe too outgoing and too likeable.

A person came to me and told me that rumors had been circulating about Bill engaging in a romantic relationship with someone who reported to him, which is a conflict of interest and a violation of company policy. I had also received reports that Bill had falsified an expense report in order to entertain this woman. That, of course, was a misappropriation of assets and a violation of company policy as well.

Now, if these allegations were true and I didn't do anything about them, they'd pose a serious challenge to my reputation as CEO. In a situation like this, you might be tempted to protect your close friend and turn your head, justifying his behavior as human nature, because men and women have attractions to other people and, it's safe to say, many people aren't always completely honest about expense reports. So it wouldn't be all that hard to question the rumors, stall, say, "Let's give this another month," and hope it all goes away. On the other hand, if you don't act on it, it could spread like a cancer. People would start saying, "I see my CEO turning a blind eye and tolerating what are violations of company policy taking place under his nose. And, therefore, I'm receiving the message from my CEO that it's okay for me to behave in the same way."

I remember, when I first got wind of the situation, I had an almost overwhelming need for solitude; I had to think. So I shut my office door, turned off my phone, and asked myself several questions: *Do I give my friend Bill the benefit of the doubt, or do I stand on principle and protect the company's interests? How quickly do I act? Could this be fixed without taking drastic measures? How broadly do I discuss the dilemma that Bill's alleged actions present? How do I handle it? What if I confront Bill and it turns out the rumors were false? How would that affect our relationship?* For me, these were not simple questions to answer.

When I emerged from my office, from my deep contemplation, I called for an investigation. I brought in my VP of human resources and another team member, who I trusted completely, and they were able to access expense reports and email records, both of which were company property. We conducted a little back-channel validation to determine what was on the expense report and whether Bill was indeed engaged in an improper romantic entanglement. In this particular case, the investigation was condemning.

I had to fire Bill the very next day.

I chose to fire Bill myself rather than have someone else do the deed, even though he did not report to me. He was, after all, a friend, and I thought he should hear the news from me directly. More importantly, I felt I owed it to the company. I owed it to the people who observed this inappropriate behavior to see tangible evidence that I took it seriously and that I personally wielded the termination axe.

Bill's violation of company policy justified my decision; however, I assumed the role of executioner with something much more important in mind. As Jeff Pinneo said, fusing an organization together around a culture of mutual respect "is precious when you have it [and] destroys you if you don't." Nothing unravels the fusion process more quickly than an executive who clearly acts on behalf of his or her own selfish interest. People identify this immediately. It's like a cancer cell invading an otherwise healthy body. Left unchecked, this type of behavior begins to communicate the opposite message from that conveyed by Fusion Leaders: that employees are there, toiling away every day to generate more power, wealth, and privilege for the executives. Talk about deflating an organization! If this is the message coming from the top, most employees will become clock punchers who don't connect to the mission and certainly don't identify themselves with the collective ego.

I remember sitting down with Bill on a warm summer afternoon to tell him as succinctly as possible about the investigation and to say, "Bill, I'm here to fire you." Because he was a friend and a top performer who was bringing in substantial revenue despite the economic downturn and because he had no idea there had been an investigation going on, he was thunderstruck. I'm fairly certain he thought that, because of our friendship, I'd give him a break. He immediately denied the charges, and when I assured him that our probe had come up with some condemning evidence and that I wasn't going to budge in my decision, he started to become threatening. "I'm getting a lawyer, and you'll pay for this, Dudley!" he said, or words to that effect.

It was a tough afternoon.

But it was worth it; it was the right thing to do. And it didn't take long before word reverberated out and around the company—that I engaged in this face-to-face showdown, even though I didn't have to do it myself. What's more, some of Bill's peers, as well as his subordinates, later approached me to say how grateful they were to see that I was willing to defend the company's interests and make the hard and somewhat awkward decision to fire a leader, a rainmaker, and a friend. I'm now several years out of the company, and I still hear about it.

We were operating in the teeth of the recession and under enormous pressure to generate results and drive performance. To have to show one of my top performers the door was not something I wanted to do. But the decision reflects four key tenets of handling a crisis through Fusion Leadership: Cultivate trust (in this case, in my HR team and in myself), maintain and enhance credibility, exercise transparency, and, of course, be clear about who owns the crisis.

CHAPTER 5

HOW MUCH DO YOU PAY YOURSELF AND OTHERS?

SHOW TRANSPARENCY AND BAKE A BIGGER PIE: CREATING A COMPENSATION STRUCTURE THAT ENCOURAGES COLLABORATION

Ask people who know Leslie Braksick, and they'll likely characterize her as an optimist, through and through. It seems she's been seen that way since her youth, when she was named the most cheerful girl in her high school, and, to this day, she calls herself a glass-half-full kind of person.

And why wouldn't she? She has many good reasons to be happy.

Braksick cofounded what quickly became an extremely successful management-consulting firm, the Continuous Learning Group Inc., leading CLG as its chairman and president/CEO for almost fifteen years and advising the firm's most senior clients for some twenty-one years. As part of a planned succession strategy, she stepped down from that company to cofound and manage her current one, My Next Season, a consulting firm that's described well by its tagline: *executives transitioning from productivity to purpose.*

In addition to consulting and executive coaching, Braksick is an entrepreneur, author, and educator, as well as a keynote speaker and board member. She and her husband of twenty-five years live in a comfortable home outside of Pittsburgh—consistently ranked as one of the nation's most livable cities—and have two children. What's more, she's highly educated, holding a doctoral degree in applied behavior science, a master's in industrial and organizational psychology, and a second master's degree from Johns Hopkins University Bloomberg School of Public Health.

Clearly, this is a woman who has accomplished a lot, enjoys a fulfilling life, and sees a bright future on the horizon. But like all of us, Braksick has experienced her share of setbacks, disappointments, and unhappiness.

Three eye-opening and negative experiences taught her a lot and motivated her to take the career path she carved out for herself. The first hit her hard and, because she has a very empathetic personality, left her heart heavy.

I want to recount this and the two other incidents that Braksick shared with me, because they reveal a lot about her but also because, in the larger scheme of things, they reflect the sometimes stark and harsh reality of the work world. Perhaps more relevant to the subject of this book, they also helped shape her leadership style, which I think falls well within the realm of Fusion Leadership.

But before I do, let me tell you more about Braksick. The first book she wrote, *Unlock Behavior, Unleash Profits: Developing Leadership Behavior that Drives Profitability in Your Organization*, earned critical acclaim and made *The Wall Street Journal*'s Business Best Seller list. She's also the author of *Preparing CEOs for Success: What I Wish I Knew*, for which she interviewed more than two dozen CEOs, getting them to reveal some very candid thoughts, strategies, and observations about their lives and careers. Reviewers also heaped praise on her work, including one who hailed it as a "breakthrough book" about business leadership.

For years, many people had been noticing Braksick's accomplishments, but in 2002, she began receiving more formal honors. That's the year she was recognized as one of the top fifty business leaders in Pennsylvania, named as a Woman of Spirit by Carlow College (now called Carlow University), and honored as a

Pittsburgh Pacesetter in Business. In 2006, she received the Athena Award from Athena International, which recognizes excellence in professional and community leadership. Four years later, in 2010, Western Michigan University bestowed on her a Distinguished Alumni Award, which mirrored what she'd earned a year earlier from the College of Arts and Sciences.

Leadership Key: Keep an Open Book

I mentioned that CLG gained success quickly. That may be an understatement, as Braksick, her partner, and her team of consultants pulled in $1.2 million in their first ten months and then doubled revenues every year after that for the next five or six years. And she led her firm in the right way.

"Yes, we were very successful right away," she said, "and I think a large part of that centers around doing what you say, saying what you do, and acting honestly and with transparency. That was always our operating philosophy as a company, and I think it's what allowed us to be so successful so soon in a very crowded market."

While I could have included Braksick and her leadership experience in virtually any one of the chapters of this book, I chose to ask for her contribution on the subject of compensation. That is, how much should leaders pay themselves in relation to the others in their organizations? What tenets should guide a leader and an organization when it comes to compensation?

For Braksick, one of the guiding principles in this regard has to do with what she mentioned above: acting honestly and with transparency. At CLG, when it came to who gets paid what, she and her team laid all the cards on the table. People knew what their colleagues earned—and she wouldn't have it any other way. "We published it," she said, referring to salaries. "We were very open about it."

Braksick has a lot to offer on the subject of compensation, and she was quite generous and candid with me about a topic that can be delicate and difficult to discuss for many people. I know that I faced internal turmoil about the many complexities that come with compensation, which I get to in the subsequent pages. But let's get back to those three experiences that shaped Braksick's career and outlook on life.

Pivotal Incidents that Proved Revelatory

As an undergraduate in the 1980s, Braksick had her sights set on a graduate program in clinical psychology. To prepare herself for that, she spent the summer before her junior year working as a camp counselor in a center that helped people with mental and physical disabilities. What she encountered—again, in part because of her empathetic nature—deeply distressed her. "I found myself overwhelmed and saddened by the circumstances the folks there found themselves in and realized I was no longer a cheerful person," she recalls. "My empathy overwhelmed my ability to process [the circumstances of the people she counseled]. So I realized that my career plan wasn't going to work; I needed to find something else."

This first career-changing experience led to another, one that pushed her steps closer to the occupational trajectory she would eventually travel and closer to designing and implementing a compensation model that fused her staff together.

The semester after working as a camp counselor, she studied abroad, in London, and took a course called The Psychology of Work. She was easily the youngest person in the class, which had several different types of workers, from doctors and lawyers to tradespeople. Despite her classmates' obvious differences, she noticed a common denominator they shared, a disheartening one: Their jobs made them miserable.

"They were angry, and they were frustrated," she said. "Each one of them had what seemed to me to be very legitimate issues with their workplace, whether it was a person who was doing the same work as somebody alongside them but getting paid twice as much as they were or, more often, people who were doing half the amount of work but were being paid the same amount. Some of my classmates complained about being promised promotions but not given promotions. These were people who were asked to do double the amount of work with no compensation change. Everyone had their story, and each one of their stories struck me as very legitimate."

Braksick became fascinated with the question of who actually fixes these things in the workplace. She also understood the significance of this extreme career dissatisfaction—given that people spend the majority of their time at work—and the far-reaching ramifications of it. "If they're angry, they're going to go home, and they're going to parent angrily," she said. "They're going to be frustrated people in the world."

This got her wondering about who would tell an angry person's boss that a situation or relationship in the workplace was causing such debilitating infuriation and, no doubt, cutting into productivity. Who would help them have the tough conversation with his or her coworker? So she set out to find who does that—what field exists in the world where somebody could go into the business world and have honest conversations about things that need to change and then help them make those changes. What she discovered was industrial psychology, and that's the area in which she earned both a master's and a doctoral degree.

During her postgraduate education at Western Michigan University, she also worked as an internal consultant for the college and published several of her written works. Upon graduation, she received some great job offers, and this is what led to the third experience that moved her career along and helped inspire her to embrace a leadership model that's very much like Fusion Leadership.

One of Braksick's job prospects looked especially promising, as it was a position with a well-known, successful consulting firm where she could earn a very good income. She interviewed—I'm guessing she interviewed quite well—and reinterviewed, and because the company was making her a generous, we-want-you-badly offer, she decided to question the partners about a couple of things. "I asked them how they structure the work with their clients and how the projects were set up," she said.

"They said, 'Well, here is what we sell to the clients, and then here is what we actually do. We sell based on our big names, senior people, and then we staff it with people like you, entry-level people.'

"I said, 'Do you ever explain that to the client?'

"They said, 'No, no, no, because we wouldn't sell the project then. They're really buying the big names, but this is how we make our margins.'

"They went through it all, and I said, 'Well, isn't it unethical not to be upfront with the client from the outset?'

"They said, 'No, this is how the game is played, and this is how things work.' I left there convinced that was not the place for me, because it seemed so unethical."

Braksick went on to interview with another big, prestigious consultancy, where one of the senior partners told her what a great culture the company had, how they supported one another, worked collaboratively, and enjoyed a great camaraderie. "They offered me very, very good money to go work there," Braksick says. "But then I met with another senior partner, and he proceeded to trash the person I'd just met with. So, again, I was struck by it. I left there thinking that just being good at what you do, being ethical, and being truly collegial might differentiate you in the consulting field."

Then, at the ripe old age of twenty-seven, when Braksick was actually hoping to mentor under some very smart, senior, accomplished organizational consultants, she ended up cofounding CLG with another woman, Dr. Julie Smith, who had an educational background identical to Braksick's but was five years her senior. "It was not my intent to start CLG when we did," she said. "It really came as a result of my being so utterly unimpressed with what else was out there in the marketplace that I thought, 'My gosh, with a little bit of effort, we could do it so much better.'"

When Braksick told me about this job interviewing experience, I'd like to say I was shocked. But I wasn't. Many service businesses—from consultancies to law partnerships and accounting firms—do operate with bait-and-switch tactics, promising that senior people will handle the clients' accounts and then quietly assigning those accounts to junior associates, saving internal costs and generating more profit. Sadly, the partner was right when he or she told Braksick that this is just the way the game is played—at least, it is all too often. In addition, it's not uncommon for partners to bad-mouth one another, although they usually don't show that ugly side to potential new hires; they wait until you're officially onboard to talk trash. And similar unsavory practices go on with companies that make products, too, of course.

Fostering Trust and Teamwork

As I said, these three pivotal experiences—the frustration and melancholy of working with the disabled and feeling helpless to substantially improve their lives, the London classroom revelation that so many workers hate their jobs, and the disillusionment with the status quo following two interview debacles—led Braksick to change her career plans and cultivate her own leadership approach. A key component of that approach is the central issue of this chapter: compensation.

When Braksick and Smith set up the salary structure for themselves and their colleagues at CLG, they analyzed the research that's been conducted on compensation, reading and synthesizing as much as they could. They concluded that the best combination of compensation has three components to it: individual contributions, team contributions, and organizational contributions. They constructed their pay package along these lines.

"The point was you couldn't maximize your total possible earnings unless all three of those goals, if you will, were met," she said. "So if a person did outstanding as an individual but the team wasn't successful and the organization wasn't successful, they couldn't reach their max. Or if they were not successful individually but the team had a banner year, they couldn't max. We really tried to tie behaviors and consequences by designing people's compensation, including mine as CEO, with those three components."

In my opinion, this model breeds trust and collaboration, and when people believe in one another and work together to achieve common goals, they can accomplish a lot. I asked Braksick if this compensation philosophy was a huge focus of CLG because she,

Smith, and their team knew the company had the potential to be very successful financially. "Yes, that's right, and we had to structure it in a way that would allow everyone to benefit from that," she said. "If a senior person had a base of $100,000, my compensation base as a partner and co-owner of the firm was $110,000, and our managing partner who ran the firm for the first couple of years [before Braksick became CEO] was at $130,000. Those are real [1990s] numbers. So we always believed in the player–coach model, but we never had huge discrepancies between us."

That's fascinating to me, because I applied almost the exact same percentages to answer the question *How much do I pay myself versus the senior executives who report to me?* Braksick echoed my own thinking when she added, "People appreciated that [relatively equitable structure], because we were kind of in this thing together. It shouldn't be just because of a title that you're paid so much more." I'll discuss this more later.

Now, don't think that everything at CLG was "all Cadillacs and smiles," to borrow a phrase from the great writer James McBride. Braksick and Smith encountered some pushback. The older consultants, the seasoned people, were accustomed to having a more guaranteed income. Consequently, they grumbled and groaned about having so much compensation at risk. "I would say the biggest pressure point we always faced in terms of compensation," Braksick said, "was that the senior people always wanted a higher percentage of guaranteed income. It was as if they felt they had it coming; it was owed to them because of their seniority."

In the mid-1990s, when CLG was getting started and growing, some of the people Braksick and Smith were recruiting worked at other companies and were used to making $200,000. She and Smith would offer them $100,000 as a base salary, $50,000 in billing bonus earnings potential, $50,000 in billing potential for their team success, and $50,000 based on the organization's success. So they had the ability to earn $250,000, which, of course, is $50,000 more than the $200,000—but only $100,000 of that was guaranteed.

"They didn't like it; they just didn't like it," she said. "They felt that there were factors they couldn't control. But I really liked the contingent relationship of compensation, the idea that they couldn't max if they weren't contributing or the team wasn't winning or the organization wasn't successful. That was always a hard sell, so we inevitably found ourselves negotiating a base of $120,000 [or so], and it was always a pressure point. I can't remember hiring any senior person who came in and said, 'That sounds like a good idea to me.'"

So CLG would bend a little but not bend over backward to accommodate the preferences of these experienced workers. And although it might have been tempting and a lot less stressful for Braksick to yield to this pushback—and perhaps her selfish ego might have wanted to avoid the confrontation with the consultants— she didn't give in much. Either the consultants worked within this model or they could work for another consultancy that had a more typical arrangement.

$$$—A Hot-Button Issue

But let me back up in time to 1993, when Braksick and Smith cofounded the original company and how the next several years played out, because this, I believe, is a compelling story. It serves as a clear manifestation of the principles and goals of Fusion Leadership in making compensation decisions. It also demonstrates how compensation can be a contentious, lightning-rod issue.

Braksick and Smith formed CLG with a third cofounder, a man we'll call Fred, who had been a very successful corporate executive and was twenty-five years their senior. He was impressed by the two women and what they had achieved in their career, particularly at Bell Atlantic. "He was a private consultant and coach to the CEO of Bell Atlantic and the head of learning," Braksick recalls. "He was a visionary leader who loved what we had done at Bell Atlantic, the positive impact we had made. He met with us when we were both at the non-profit, and we shared with him that we were going to leave the non-profit [to set up a new business]. He said he'd love to be our third partner, and we loved the idea of having him. He was a wonderful business partner, and the success of the company certainly was a result of the three of us founding it and leading it."

But a difference in thinking surfaced when it came to compensation—a stark difference. Braksick and Smith wanted to share equity more broadly across the company. Fred, like many corporate leaders, wanted a structure that favored the company's owners and the most senior executives when the company was bringing in good profits. "Julie and I wanted to modify the equity structure of the company so more would reap financial benefits should the company be successful. He was not supportive of that structure and felt that, as owners and founders, it was our due [to keep the equity] and choose when to share it and with whom," Braksick says.

Now, this is not a good guy/bad guy situation. It's a legitimate, understandable difference of views among top-drawer professionals who all brought important skills and experience to the business. I've seen this occur often. In fact, I encountered it firsthand at Integra Telecom and will discuss this in subsequent pages.

In 1998, five years after the company's founding, Fred expressed a desire to monetize the company's success and retire. By selling the company, the owners would reap the rewards of the success of the business, and Fred would be free to consider other career options. The two younger owners would have preferred to buy his one-third of the business and retain ownership of the firm but recognized they'd have to go into debt to do that. So they sought out buyers who would purchase the company, allow Braksick and Smith to continue to lead it, and enable Fred to move on to the next phase of his life.

Braksick and Smith gathered the employees together for a retreat in Florida, where they explained to everyone what the situation was and why they were going to sell the company. "We involved the whole company in developing the criteria for the buyer. We all brainstormed about what we wanted that to look like," Braksick says. "As CEO at that time, I made it clear not only that we would apply their criteria but also that I would continue to lead the firm post-sale. Consequently, they could hold me personally accountable for delivering on that commitment."

It's easy to see Fusion Leadership principles at work here: 1. She and Smith pulled all of the CLG's members together to formulate the purchase criteria collectively. 2. She communicated clearly that she would continue to run the firm. 3. She promised personal accountability.

Eventually, they found a buyer that would keep the company intact, Braksick signed a three-year agreement to stay on as CEO, "and we used this opportunity to enable Fred to retire," she said.

The company that bought CLG struggled in different ways, so, in her capacity as CEO, Braksick gave them a proposal to buy back the business, which they did just three years after selling it. And what do you suppose Braksick, Smith, and their senior-most colleagues did immediately on purchasing it? They instituted an equity structure that shared ownership of the company and enabled an employee stock ownership plan, recognizing that, in the long run, sharing the equity would fuse their workforce together and propel the company forward for even greater success.

"In 2001, we bought our company back, and when we did, with that original owner no longer in the picture, we instituted an employee stock ownership program that allowed everyone—every secretary, every assistant, every travel agent, every consultant—to be a shareholder of the firm," she said. "It took a while until we had the board's support to do this, but it was important to me and important to my other cofounder. Sometimes you can't do everything you want to do when you want to do it."

But she proves that—with strong leadership, dogged perseverance, and steadfast confidence that your vision is the right one—ultimately, you can prevail.

I found Braksick's story to be very stirring. It affected me because, as I said, it provides a real-world example of how much of a lightning rod this compensation philosophy issue can become in an organization. I'm not saying every organization touches this lightning rod, but I'm aware of many that do. It certainly was a hot-button topic for me and my colleagues. When I stop to think about this, I find it remarkable that it took Braksick seven-plus years to implement something that was so important to her and

Smith that they collectively chose to sell the business and buy it back as the path of least resistance to get to the outcome they sought—the flatter compensation structure.

Given the success the company went on to have, that was clearly the right move.

Experiencing the "Greater Good"

As Braksick was telling me about what she paid herself, I wondered if she ever wished she'd done what most corporate leaders do: pull rank and pull in the big bucks. Did she ever regret leaving money on the table? (I know that I've had moments where I did.)

"I can't say that I ever felt that way," she said. "I felt like we made very good money. To me, it's always about a marathon, not a sprint, and maybe it's different because I was building a service company, where it's not like you're marking up the cost of a product to make your margins. It was a knowledge service business. As we got better, we were able to command a higher rate, and the company did very well financially. As a result, everybody benefitted, including me."

Her strategy . . . wait, let me amend that. Her extremely successful, very smart strategy on compensation structure was intended to inspire others, to make sure they understood that they're "all in this together," as she puts it, and "to see the greater good and larger benefit." As a result, CLG baked a bigger pie for everyone, even though the piece of the pie she as the CEO carved out for herself was only slightly larger than others, she would be well off financially because the organization succeeded collectively.

When I mentioned the pie metaphor, Braksick jumped on it: "That was the exact language I was about to use. My goal has always been to create a bigger pie. It's hard-wired in me. I love creating the bigger pie. And I love to create wealth for many people. Now, in my current company, we give 20 percent of our revenue to not-for-profits, because I want to role-model giving back in significant ways and making a difference, and so you have to have money to do that. To give back in a bold and meaningful way, you have to have money. I always felt like I was more than fairly compensated for what I did, and, because I had the position of authority and ability, my goal was always to make the pie bigger and benefit from that."

By applying this philosophy, the short-sighted selfish ego bites the dust, and the long-term collective ego prevails. And that's Fusion Leadership in action.

THE COMPENSATION CORNERSTONE: SHAPING WORKPLACE BEHAVIOR WITH A HIGHLY VISIBLE TOOL

Everything was in place for a wonderful evening. My wife, Laurie, and I were sitting down to an intimate dinner party at some good friends' house, with other good friends attending. One of the side benefits of running a company like Integra Telecom and then, subsequently, serving on corporate boards and getting deeply involved in professional associations is that I get to meet and befriend a lot of charismatic, successful CEOs of other companies. The host of the party—I'll call him Ted—is one of those corporate leaders. He built, ran, and then sold a very successful business and became quite wealthy in the process.

Ted and his wife had gone all out for this casual yet elegant affair in their beautiful home in one of Portland's more exclusive neighborhoods. We drank incredible bottles of wine, ate delicious gourmet food, and talked and laughed. Everyone was having a great time.

Except for me. I felt tense, with my neck stiff, my palms clammy, and my stomach clenched. I felt out of sorts.

I'll explain why shortly. But first, let me get to one of the central points of this chapter by referring to the song "Money" by the band Pink Floyd, which was one of their big hits of the 1970s. In it, they sing about money-grabbing, buying luxury items, and the allure of lavish wealth. Those of you who know this song—from the iconic

Dark Side of the Moon album—can probably hear the cash register pings that Pink Floyd laced into the music to add emphasis to the catchy lyrics written by Roger Waters.

Let's be honest. Most of us—maybe all of us?—want to drive nice cars, live in beautiful homes, travel to exotic destinations, and live the proverbial good life. You want money, and I want money. I certainly did when I ran Integra Telecom. I also wanted the company to succeed, my leadership team to prosper, and all of our employees to earn a better-than-decent salary, provide well for their families, live in a nice home, and put aside a college fund for their kids. And, indeed, we did accomplish those goals. I made sure of that.

But I struggled, mightily, with a critical question that anyone who's in the position to help set compensation levels must ask, answer, and act on accordingly: *How much do I pay myself?* As Leslie Braksick demonstrated at her consulting firm, as articulated in the previous pages, compensation represents one of the most tangible forms of evidence of whether the CEO is serious and committed to the idea of managing under the Fusion Leadership model and creating a culture of mutual respect. For many CEOs—dare I say a vast majority of CEOs—their strong desire to generate personal wealth determines their company's compensation configuration. In fact, in many ways, the top-down hierarchical leadership structure and style they buy into and operate under dictates that they *should* earn significantly more than their senior vice presidents and hundreds of times more than their frontline employees.

At many companies, CEO compensation is out of control and, in my opinion, a significant source of employee unrest. Consider this example from a 2010 ABCNews.go.com report: "The CEO of Walmart earns more in an hour than his employees will earn in a year. . . . Walmart CEO Michael Duke's $35 million salary, when converted to an hourly wage, worked out to $16,826.92. By comparison, at a Walmart store planned for [Chicago's] Pullman neighborhood, new employees to be paid $8.75 an hour would gross $13,650 [sic] a year." I can't help but think that it's no wonder Walmart has experienced such a backlash from their employees and received hard hits from the media.

Think that's an extreme example? Hardly. Consider this 2014 headline from cbsnews.com: "Fast-food CEOs make one thousand times more than their workers." Again, with this kind of compensation discrepancy, it's no surprise that fast-food workers have been staging strikes and executing walkouts.

Of course, companies like Walmart and those in the fast-food industry are not the norm. But vast income gaps, albeit not as large as those examples, do exist in nearly every economic sector; the auto industry comes to mind. Let me also say, I'm a capitalist. Many of these Fortune 500 CEOs are gifted leaders who deserve a lot. By employing tens of thousands of people and managing the economic engines that drive our developed world, they bring incredible value to our community. They certainly deserve to make more than our favorite pro athletes, who play games for a living.

In terms of CEO compensation compared to the next-highest leader in the company, it's quite common for the chief to earn more than two, three, four, or more times than his or her second- and third-in-command. In my opinion, that's too much. As Integra Telecom's CEO, I took the view that if you put yourself on a financial pedestal, where you're making two or three times the pay of the people in the offices right next to yours who you say hello to every morning, you're impeding your ability to create the kind of positive and passionate workplace culture that's one of the most important goals of Fusion Leadership. I was very conscious of this.

The amount I paid myself was only about 10–15 percent higher than the next-highest-paid person in the company. That consisted of the base pay, the annual bonus, and any equity incentives. At least three managers knew this: the CFO, the COO, and the head of human resources. Our board of directors knew it, and I can safely assume that word of this leaked to other employees.

Furthermore, I had to assume that everything we did would someday be written up in the newspaper or that it would be part of a public filing. I just always embraced transparency and operated under the idea that, sooner or later, everybody's going to see what's behind the curtain. And if employees, from the lowest paid to the executive vice presidents, saw that I was making a disproportionate income, the passionate workforce that I was working hard to foster would be jeopardized. I didn't want an inflated compensation package hammering a wedge between my relationships with others. I felt that flew in the face of Fusion Leadership.

Having said that, I must be candid: I struggled with this—constantly. My selfish ego would whisper into my ear, *Dudley, you work very hard. You built this company into the successful organization that it has become. You employ thousands of people. Pay yourself more. Think of your wife and two kids. Think about that new car. Listen to the ping of the cash register. (Ping.)* (Apparently, my selfish ego is a Pink Floyd fan.) My commitment to the collective ego, of course, won out and drove my decision to spread the wealth around and downward while still allowing me to earn a handsome income.

Back to the Party: Tense and Nervous

So, as I sat at the dinner party in Ted's beautiful home and listened to him and his wife talk about some exotic vacation to Aruba or Fiji or the French Riviera or wherever they'd gone that month, and as I scanned the walls and admired the huge abstract painting by one of New York's latest art superstars and the portrait of some regal-looking people and the original drawings from Australian aborigine tribesmen, and as I sipped on a vintage French Bordeaux, my hands got sweatier, my chest tightened further, and my mind continued to roam away from what I'm sure was a scintillating conversation.

And then it hit me. I knew what was causing my anxiety. I was jealous. Ted had more money than I did.

I'm a super competitive person; I hate to lose. I'm not proud of the fact that I found myself measuring success by whether I had more money than this person. I knew that Laurie and I have traveled to some amazing places in the world and collected artwork we cherish. We buy good wine too. We've sent our kids to excellent schools. But, obviously, Ted had accumulated more wealth than I had, and that was really tough for me to digest. As I sat there at this dinner, I realized I was engaged in an internal struggle, an almost schizophrenic debate in my mind. I was looking at both sides of the argument and asking the question *Was my approach to compensation the right one?*

Eventually, I was able to quiet the selfish ego, who kept saying, *You idiot. You left all that money on the table. You could have a lot more money than Ted. Why didn't you take more for yourself when you could have?* I settled into the satisfying reality that I did exactly the right thing. After all, if I hadn't made the investment in these other company leaders, Integra Telecom never would've grown so big. My company grew to be literally twenty times larger than Ted's local company ever did. And while at least twelve people at Integra Telecom became millionaires off the stock of the company and hundreds more earned more-than-respectable incomes and received bonuses and stock—all of which I'm very proud of—I'm pretty certain Ted was the only person who made a lot of money in his business. I'm also quite sure that the work environment he created wasn't nearly as collegial and team centered as Integra Telecom's. So it's okay that I didn't have as much money as Ted and his family, because I was able to share wealth with all these other people, giving me a strong sense of intangible, nonmaterialistic career satisfaction.

In the end, I made the right decision . . . I think. See? I've not completely resolved this, and I must say, it's the hardest topic in the entire book to discuss. But I do feel validated about my decisions regarding compensation on learning that Leslie Braksick—with all of her experience, academic training, and success—understood the importance of compensation and the message it sends and stood firm in her decision to set up CLG's equitable pay structure.

My compensation strategy was also difficult to talk about, not to mention implement, when I was Integra Telecom's CEO. I got a lot of criticism, in various forms, from subtle raised eyebrows and questioning looks to more blatant pushback.

I remember sitting down with a board member named Jim at our Sacramento, California, office to review the stock pool and for me to tell him how I intended to divvy it up to the employees.

Jim worked for one of the big private equity firms that invested in Integra Telecom and chaired the compensation committee of the board. While CEOs have tremendous discretion, these types of critical compensation decisions need to be approved by their boards of directors. When I told him how and to whom I planned to distribute the stock, he challenged me. He said, "Gee, most of the companies we invest in only spread this among three to five people. What you're recommending here is very different from that. You're going quite deep in your organization with dozens and dozens of people and, in some cases, hundreds of people getting a slice of the pie."

I defended my position and got my way because, as long as the overall size of the pool is the same, investors ultimately don't really care, provided that the management team is happy, the CEO supports the distribution pattern, and the other shareholders are taken care of. If that's all in place, they'll let you do whatever you want. Now, Jim wasn't the first person who forced me to defend my decision. I had similar discussions over the years with other big investors. And every time I got into this discussion with large institutional investors, I encountered the same reaction. It wasn't surprising, because they invest in dozens of companies and see lots of different approaches to compensation by the various CEOs. I concluded that my philosophy differed from that of most of my counterparts. But I stood firm—despite my ongoing internal struggle, which, as I've noted, I still deal with.

Even people on my leadership team challenged me. Three or four executives who I talked to about these allocations would argue with me. "By the time you spread the stock pool out to hundreds of people, there's just not that much," they told me. "When you get down to the lower rungs of the ladder, what they're getting is relatively small. So why do you do it?"

My response was, "I think it *is* meaningful. It might be enough for them to buy a new car or to create or bulk up a college fund. For a lot of midlevel managers, that would be a big deal for them."

After all, if we hit our numbers and the company performed like we expected it to, and it usually did, that "small" allocation could be worth $20,000 or $30,000. That's not hundreds of thousands, but it's still a lot of money. The long-term benefit extends a long way, because sharing the riches allows you to look people in the eye and say, "If you contribute toward this greater cause, we're all going to benefit. We'll all get a share in the wealth creation. That message, I thought and still do think, is powerful.

I came to learn that this compensation philosophy was fairly unusual. But when I spoke to Darrell Cavens, the CEO of the e-retail company Zulily, he expressed pride at the number of millionaires he helped create. He measures his own success, in part, on this metric. I had not heard anyone else take pride in that measure. That really resonated with me and, in some ways, constitutes a validation for me and relieves (at least somewhat) my internal struggle.

Singing from the Rooftop

But honestly, I still have days when I wonder if I should be a wealthier person, if maybe I went too far in the direction of spreading the wealth around, and if I'm too Pollyannaish in my view about the impact of compensation on the morale and collegiality of the workforce. Ted's party is a perfect example of one of those days.

And then, on the other hand, I experience something that makes me want to go stand on a rooftop and sing about how good I feel about what I did, sharing the wealth, and how personally fulfilling that is. That's how I felt when I got an email from Lori, a manager in the company's Prior Lake, Minnesota, office, some twenty miles south of the Twin Cities.

Lori contacted me—just a few weeks after Ted's party, by the way—because she was retiring after thirty-six years of working for Integra Telecom and SRT, the company Integra Telecom acquired. At her retirement party, the night before she wrote to me, she spoke about the ten or so things that stood out during her time with the company, and she wanted to share that list of highlights with me. They included things like the first time the company offered Internet access, fun-filled and collegial company barbecues, a major office move, and a promotion where she gained responsibility for a larger number of people, among other highlights.

One of Lori's fond memories came in 2003. It was a tough year, as the nation faced many economic challenges, and Integra Telecom was struggling to meet its numbers. She reminded me—and I'd forgotten about this—that because the company was just treading water, I decided that the top executives at Integra Telecom would not receive any bonuses that year. We would use that money to strengthen the company's financial position and, in effect, fund the bonus pool for managers and frontline workers. Because everybody was working hard to get through the tough times, I delighted in announcing that we would still pay bonuses to everyone except the senior people; the midlevel managers all the way down to the frontline people would all get paid.

Here is Lori in her own words: "I want to thank you from the bottom of my heart for all you've done for SRT and Integra Telecom. You definitely took us to the next level, or three or four. I especially remember the time when you came to Prior Lake to announce that Integra Telecom did not meet budget, and you and others gave up your bonus payments so that we may have ours. I am sure you gave up much more than that in order to take care of the employees. I highly respect you for that and appreciate all you did for the employees; I noticed it quite often. I enjoyed working under your direction."

I read that email and climbed up on my roof and started singing—metaphorically speaking, of course. It made me proud that someone I hadn't talked to in many years remembered my executive decision, listed it as a highlight of her tenure at Integra Telecom, and made sure to share her memory with me.

I've talked about the ripple effect several times in these pages, that highly visible act or behavior that is talked about and retold many, many times, causing reverberations throughout the organization. I think the decision to forgo senior leadership bonuses but pay everyone else represents another manifestation of that phenomenon. This management move resonated broadly across the organization, because each of the regional senior vice presidents didn't receive a bonus; the decision was talked about in staff meetings across our eleven states. I'm fairly certain that it carried a tremendous impact, sending very clear communication to employees that company leaders recognized that they were working hard that year, that they had done a lot to move the company forward. The senior leaders were focused on the health of the company—at that time, a lot of companies were going bankrupt—and we needed to do what was right for Integra Telecom in the long term. But we did not want to do it on the backs of our middle management and frontline workers. I think we conveyed the message that we were dedicated to the success of our people and that the notion of a shared commitment started with us.

Your team will devour and digest every morsel of information relating to compensation, making it highly visible and a critical tool in driving human behavior and fusing your organization together. While these stories focus on salaries, bonuses, and stock compensation, leaders must consider all the valuable tools to consider in the compensation landscape. The metrics you measure and the behaviors you reward in setting bonus targets, the amount of compensation "at risk" compared to the amount "guaranteed" in one's salary, how to structure a sales incentive plan, how often to pay bonuses, and how deeply to extend incentive compensation into a work force—these are but a few of the issues good leaders constantly mull over. Fortunately, much has been written on these topics, and I will leave the tactics of relating compensation to organizational behavior and reward systems to others. The challenge to the Fusion Leader, as always, lies in the struggle between your selfish interests and what is best for the organization.

I'd like to end this chapter with a point of emphasis and some advice. First, it's important for leaders to understand that setting compensation is one of the most tangible decisions you make in terms of the kind of environment you're creating. I would advise you to ask yourself and the people around you what compensation approach to take. You need to find the right middle place. You want to be confident that you're not making the mistake of slipping into the power leadership structure, where it's all about you. That's something you want to avoid at all costs—that is, if you agree with and want to subscribe to the Fusion Leadership model.

On reflection, I should add that I'm not sure if people need to go as far as I went. It's okay to take care of yourself and to reap the rewards of your hard work and the wealth that's created by a successful company. There's nothing wrong with that, so find a compensation arrangement that's right for you and ensures that you stay on the right side of the line, allowing Fusion Leadership to flourish. And it will be different from company to company. The way I did it isn't necessarily the way everybody should do it. You need to land on the place where you can look your colleagues in the eye and explain in a very confident and self-assured way why you're setting the compensation the way you are. Your clarity on how much to pay yourself and how much to pay others cements the cornerstone in building a culture of mutual respect.

CHAPTER 6

HOW DO YOU MOTIVATE EMPLOYEES TO MANIFEST THE VISION?

DRIVING THE VISION: P&G LEADER PUSHED CHANGE TO BOOST REVENUES AND ENHANCE COLLABORATION

Late in the year 2000, change circulated in the air within the boardrooms of one of the most well-known corporations in the world, and one of its top executives served as the chief agent of that change. As president of Procter & Gamble's vast Asia–India–Australia market, Chip Bergh ran the regional operations from the company's Asian headquarters thirty-plus floors up, in the regal Gateway Towers in Singapore. On a clear day, Bergh could see three countries—Malaysia, Indonesia, and, of course, Singapore—from his posh, expansive C-suite office. "I overlooked the harbor in Singapore, and the view was spectacular," he recalled. "It was a beautiful office."

In essence, it was the type of work environment many people lust after. But not Bergh. In fact, he helped lead the charge out of that desirable workspace and into more modest accommodations.

At the time, Cincinnati-based Procter & Gamble, the multinational consumer-goods manufacturer, was reorganizing itself with a keen eye toward Asia's growth potential. P&G had tapped Bergh to lead the transformation, and he arrived committed to extending the P&G vision into this vast market. That meant creating a new regional Asia headquarters organization, boosting its Singapore workforce from about seventy employees to some seven hundred, with P&G people coming in from around the region, and finding ways to cut costs. Consequently, they moved the Asian regional headquarters into a building called Novena Square, which was *not* right on the water, *not* thirty-plus floors up, and *not* with a spectacular view of three countries. "I actually had a view of a hospital out the back window, and we were over a mall on the front side," Bergh said. "Simply put, it was less expensive real estate."

The move to cheaper digs and the major increase in the workforce, however, weren't the only changes. Bergh, intent on energizing Asia to become Procter & Gamble's next growth engine, decided to dispense with the traditional office layout, opting instead for an open-space setting with no offices behind doors and walls. He also adopted the concept of *hot desking*, a model some consultancies and cutting-edge companies had been experimenting with at the time but one that was foreign to Procter & Gamble. Essentially, the seven hundred employees would share five hundred desks, often a different desk in a different space on different days. This would work, Bergh figured, because people were traveling a lot or taking vacations, so the staff was always at about 70-percent capacity anyway. They would share desks, the company would operate more efficiently, and the employees would work more as a team or in groups of teams.

The office remodel really shook things up. But it was driven by a few common-sense factors. "First, it was a recognition that everybody doesn't need an office five days a week, because of the traveling schedules we had," he explained. "Number two, the model saved us the equivalent of a full floor. That is, if we had a desk for every single person, we would need another floor, which would cost another $2 million a year. Number three, it would create this culture of collaboration and agility and speed by having people sitting with their logical work teams on a day-in and day-out basis, with no walls separating them."

People in the corporate facilities department made sure they designed enough space for private phone calls and face-to-face meetings. "There's a whole ecosystem you have to build in when you do an open office," Bergh said. "You have to make sure the phones are mobile so, when you get a phone call, you can duck into a huddle room. And I had experts who knew about these certain design elements."

Bergh said the underpinning of this operational makeover "was partly financial and partly pragmatic, and the objective was to use it as this new culture of vibrancy, versus everybody sitting in offices with their doors closed most of the time."

So everyone embraced the reorganization, went with the flow, accepted their boss's imposition of this sweeping transformation because, hey, change is good, right? Wrong. Many resisted.

Fusion Leaders Must Advance the Vision

I'll convey what Bergh told me about the resistance he encountered and how he dealt with it. But first, let me offer a little context.

Bergh served as a top executive at Procter & Gamble for several years before becoming the CEO of Levi Strauss, the position he held when I met him in 2014 at the Ernst & Young National Entrepreneur of the Year Strategic Growth Forum. He impressed me with his successful and responsible stewardship of the famous blue jean and clothing company, his highly principled approach to running a business, and his effective and service-oriented style of managing people, all of which are attributes that I think fall clearly into the camp of Fusion Leadership.

Perhaps what struck me the most—and continues to resonate with me—is Bergh's vision. (Some readers may remember that president George Bush, the elder, would talk about developing the "vision thing," something comedic impersonators had fun with, particularly Dana Carvey from *Saturday Night Live*. But I digress.) All leaders must be forward-thinking, capable of projecting and, to some extent, shaping the future. Bergh knew, however, that articulating a vision was not, by itself, enough. Throughout his career, he learned that only after you fuse an organization together can you realize your opportunity to truly lead. That's when it's time to lead the charge and when your organization is positioned to follow. You can visualize the future all you want, but if you can't find a way to make that vision manifest, you're, in essence, living a fantasy. Bergh envisioned what path he wanted his employees to take, and then he designed it, built it, and led them along that path—with great success.

The overhaul of the Singapore office model illustrates one example of Bergh's vision. A key linchpin to making it succeed was his decision to work out of a cubicle just like his employees. His desk was exactly the same size as everyone else's, and it sat out on the floor with the frontline workers. I know why he did this—for many of the same reasons I worked right alongside my Integra Telecom employees in Minneapolis and Colleen Abdoulah worked with the installation crews of WOW! and General Robert Van Antwerp crawled around in the Saudi desert mud to wash military vehicles: It helps create a shared organizational mission and an atmosphere that says, *We're all in this together.*

Naturally, Bergh could have occupied a traditional office, because he was, after all, the boss. "But I didn't think that was the right thing to do," he said. "I wanted to be out in the center of the action just like everybody else."

Additionally, he gave up his cubicle when he wasn't in the office, which was frequently because he traveled about 60 percent of the time. He did hold on to the rights to use his desk when he was on site. "Now, unlike most other people, if I were in the office, I had that desk," he said. "It was right next to my assistant. But anybody could have that desk when I was traveling."

As I mentioned, there was, predictably, a bit of pushback to the change. For example, some people were thrown off by Bergh's egalitarian approach; it ran contrary to everything they knew about top-down, rank-and-file management. "A lot of [the employees] could not initially accept the Big Boss, the president of the region, not having his own office," he told me. "It was like—'You're sitting out on the floor, just like everybody else?!' They had a really hard time dealing with it. Now, Procter & Gamble has adopted it globally as the office standard. In fact, even the executive floor in Cincinnati moved to an open-office plan about ten years ago. But back then, especially in Asia, the car you drove, the watch you wore, the pen you used, and the size of your office all mattered."

So this concept—the president of the region working in a cubicle the same size as his assistant's—was a very difficult one for some people to wrap their minds around. They actually thought Bergh was jeopardizing his own status inside P&G.

And, of course, several people disliked the new model, not because of their concern about how it would affect Bergh's standing within the company but because of how it affected them on a daily basis. "Some of the resistance came from ex-pats, people who grew up in the United States or Europe and were more senior people," Bergh said. "They were used to and really liked having their own offices. They probably had a harder time than most of the local people."

But you know what? Bergh didn't particularly care if the change didn't sit well with some of his colleagues. Or, put another way, he told them, in so many words, to keep an open mind, because he knew that the new office configuration was central to his vision for enhanced collaboration, growth in market share, and increased revenues and profits. "At the end of the day, I was like, 'Get over it. Give it a shot. The worst that happens is we have to add a few offices at some point.' And, in fact, people did get over it, very quickly."

It's All about Results—Both Financial and Intangible

Now I wouldn't have included this story in the book if all of this visionary thinking didn't pay dividends. Indeed, it did. The Asian region became P&G's fastest-growing business unit. Here's how Bergh described the financial success produced from the big change:

"Our business results got a lot better. Our costs were much lower than if we had given everybody an office the size that their title warranted based on the old Procter & Gamble office standards. When I got out there, the business was about $1 billion in sales, and when I left, we were close to $3 billion in sales. Now, that included the acquisition of Gillette, which, on its own, was close to $1 billion. So, organically, we probably doubled during the period of time I was there, from 2000 to 2005. We also made progress in a number of the key markets in that period. India was the most notable, where we didn't have much of a business. Before I arrived, we had sales of about $100 to $125 million. It was my fastest-growing market the last couple of years I was there." The foundation that Bergh helped build in Asia has allowed P&G to continue to grow even more in recent years and achieve even higher levels of success.

The swell of the revenue stream wasn't the only benefit realized because of the open-office arrangement. Something less tangible but equally—if not more—important occurred. Cultural collaboration and ethnic integration began to take shape fairly quickly. The regional headquarters became a global melting pot, with people from the Philippines, Thailand, Malaysia, Indonesia, Australia, New Zealand, Europe, the United States, and elsewhere working side by side and getting to know each other, putting aside racial and cultural differences.

But that didn't happen immediately. Initially, people tended to stay within their own ethnic group or country group. That's human nature. Some people knew each other before they moved in, and so they felt more comfortable hanging out with these friends and acquaintances.

Over the following six to twelve months, however, people started to integrate, and Bergh talked about it enthusiastically. "This was diversity in action," he recalled. "At one point, I think we had twenty-eight nationalities and fifty-five different languages spoken in the office. That's part of what made that concept so powerful. Within the first year, people were really beginning to make friends with those outside of their group. People became colorblind. Ethnic and cultural boundaries fell away. Within three years, we had Indians marrying Filipinos and so on. It was really cool."

For many of those employees, including the guy in charge, that Singapore experience was transcendent. "We formed a tight-knit group," Bergh said. "I left there in 2005, and ten years later, I'm still close to people from that group. A lot of us look back and say,

'That was one of the finest memories I have of my career.' We were on fire. The business results were great."

This story provides evidence that a workforce grounded in a culture of shared commitment becomes a workforce that accomplishes great things—in this case, building one of Procter & Gamble's fastest growing world markets. Being free from the tyranny of working to satisfy a power leader's ego and, instead, working to realize a common vision—that's profoundly motivating.

I asked Bergh to talk a little more about the workspace atmosphere created by the collaborative, open-office model. "We had a great culture, and it was special," he said. He then paused and added, "It was magical."

Leaving "The Pru" and Moving into the "World Shaving Headquarters"

In 2005, the brass and board at Procter & Gamble executed a major acquisition, further expanding their market by purchasing a US consumer-goods institution, the iconic razor and razor blade manufacturer Gillette. At a sale price of $57 billion, it was the biggest deal P&G had ever done.

The executives and board decided they needed Chip Bergh to help run the show, so, as he put it, he "was the first person dropped into Gillette and the most senior Procter legacy person on the ground." (Ultimately, he'd oversee the blades and razors business as president of male grooming.) *On the ground* meant in Boston, in The Prudential Building, where Gillette was headquartered—but not for long. Once again, Bergh had a vision for the future of this company, and shortly after he arrived on the scene, he started to exercise that vision.

Traditionally, Gillette employees occupied close to twenty floors of the landmark skyscraper, affectionately known as "The Pru," at a cost of more than $2 million per floor. Bergh wanted to change that with a move to South Boston, back to Gillette's roots, an old office tower on the site of the company's original plant that dates back to 1910. He wasn't the only one talking about renovating the historic building that the company already owned and moving the headquarters to this industrial neighborhood, but he strongly pushed for it. "I don't want to say it was my idea, but I saw it as an opportunity for us to reshape, restack, and reuse the existing office building by turning it into a new environment as a way to create a new culture," he said. "This was based on my experience in Singapore."

This decision would clearly disrupt employees' lives, and Bergh and his staff knew they'd meet resistance. Consider what The Pru offered its lucky inhabitants. As the most expensive real estate in Boston, it's elegant, prestigious, and centrally located. On famous Boylston Street, the tower is built on an upscale shopping mall, only two blocks from the even more famous Newbury Street. This bustling downtown urban scene has great restaurants and shopping and all the services people need, from dry cleaning to hair salons to fitness clubs. "Anything you need is a block or two blocks away," Bergh said. "And we were telling employees that we're moving out to an industrial manufacturing plant in South Boston, where there was basically nothing. People weren't so happy about this initially."

I bet not. For a lot of people, this was a significant change. They had established commuting and childcare routines and shopping patterns based on The Pru, so, naturally, the move would be disruptive. Still, Bergh and his upper management colleagues made the decision and knew they'd need to sell the idea to the employees. "I did a lot of things," he said. "For example, I played up the fact that we would have free parking, which, for some people, was a pretty significant automatic pay raise, because parking was something like $300 or $400 a month downtown."

He also convinced Procter & Gamble to put up a lot of money to transform the gritty old building into something special, a workplace that people would be proud of and one that would lend itself to the kind of dynamic, team-centered environment that Bergh created in Singapore. Bergh understood that he could not yet demand the ambitious goals he had for Gillette until he took steps to forge the workforce together, and, just as in Singapore, this new facility was a crucial first step.

"As a decision maker, I decided that, if we're going to do this, we're going to do it right," Bergh said, clearly satisfied but not boastful about what he accomplished. "I convinced Procter & Gamble to invest about $50 million to renovate and upgrade the facility that we were going to move into. We basically took an office tower in the plant that was pretty much vacant and took two years to renovate it. We built a beautiful atrium entrance. We put in Boston's best gym. We upgraded the cafeteria, which benefited everybody in the building, including the people who worked on the plant side of the facility. We upgraded not just the physical space but the quality of the food and everything else. We tried to create a new culture."

And it seems they did, indeed, do just that.

Winning Over the Workforce

The project succeeded, and Bergh captured the hearts and minds of the employees by making all the right moves. For starters, the company announced the decision far enough in advance that people had time to grieve and, if you will, get over leaving their beloved Prudential Building. Management tried to market the new site proactively, giving tours of the new space and letting employees participate in selecting the office's carpet colors and the specifics of the look of the workspace, which, of course, would be the open-office model that worked so well in Singapore. "We had a couple different workspace options," Bergh said. "We let people vote on what sort of workspace they wanted. As we got closer to the move-in date, there was more excitement and enthusiasm."

It should be noted that, like many of the employees, from the frontline workers to the managers, Bergh made sacrifices to make this move. His office high up in The Pru was a corner suite with a spectacular view. Out one side, he could look across Massachusetts Bay and watch airplanes taking off and landing at Logan International Airport. Out the other side, he could see the Charles River and the campus of the Massachusetts Institute of Technology. "I could watch the rowers going up and down the river, and I also had a gorgeous view of Cambridge and downtown Boston," he recalled. "It was beautiful. I moved into an office in South Boston that basically faced—well—South Boston, which needless to say, isn't much of a view."

What's more, his office at The Pru was only three blocks from his house, so he could walk to work in less than ten minutes. To get to the South Boston plant, he had to fight the notoriously aggressive Boston drivers, although the commute wasn't very far.

But it was worth it to Bergh, because it advanced the mission of the organization. That was easy to see from a financial savings point of view, which, naturally, helped sell the idea to the C-suite executives and the board in the first place. "We were paying about $40 million a year for office space in The Pru," Bergh explained. "I remember when I pitched the renovation of the plant office, the price tag was a little bit more than $50 million. I said, 'This is almost what we're paying for rent for one year. So it basically pays out in a little bit more than a year versus the rent that we would be continuing to pay.'"

In 2009, the inaugural year of the plant, which P&G named the World Shaving Headquarters, Bergh didn't ease off his PR efforts to reinforce to his employees that this was a smart move. He and his staff hosted a bring-your-family-to-work day, where they opened the office up for employees to show off the old/new building with its twenty-foot-ceiling, loft-style space, and ample conference and huddle rooms. They could see an Art of Shaving store that operated a real barbershop in the lobby. "We did a lot of cool stuff," he said. "We had a plant tour so people could see how razors are made. We had the cafeteria serving lunch, which the company paid for. We wanted to show off the renovated building and essentially say, 'Yes, it's not The Prudential Building a couple blocks away from Newbury Street, but we have a lot of benefits here worth celebrating.' I would say the happiness factor among employees definitely went up."

By the end of the first year, Bergh saw noticeable improvements among the workforce. Employees felt energized and production increased. They observed their boss working among them in the open-office environment and saw that he had happily given up that corner office in The Pru with the spectacular views of the bay and the river and the city. "By me being part of the rest of the crew who were giving things up, it made it fair," he told me. "I felt it was important that I was in an open office like everybody else, because that's part of how you make it work."

Having pulled the Gillette organization together, Bergh was now in a position to push performance, confident the Gillette employees were connecting to his shared vision.

Acquisition and Move Pay Off

Now, what about the results? It was imperative that Procter & Gamble's purchase of Gillette boost the company's coffers. After all, even for a multinational corporation like P&G, $57 billion is not chump change. So a lot was riding on the acquisition and the move to South Boston. Despite relocating to the World Shaving Headquarters in the middle of the Great Recession, Bergh and his team held their own. The next couple of years were "pretty good," he said. And then things started to take off.

"The Gillette blades and razor business is one of the most profitable businesses in Procter & Gamble," he said. "It's second only to the laundry business. There is little dispute within the analyst industry that the Gillette acquisition and integration was a financial success. We blew away all of the acquisition economics, and the Gillette blades and razor unit is very successful."

The culture blossomed, too, as employees embraced this new, collaborative way to work. "People were sitting in logical work groups," he said. "There was more energy and more teamwork inside the business. We built it to generate a high-performing collaborative culture, and it worked. We really got it right."

This success story didn't go unnoticed by Corporate America insiders. It's no wonder that, a few years later, a forward-thinking company like Levi Strauss & Co. came calling for Chip Bergh and hired him as their president and CEO. Talk about good moves.

MISSION WORK: LEADING BY EXAMPLE TO PUSH THE LOCAL MARKET AND DEMAND RESULTS

In the autumn of 2002, in Salt Lake City, Utah, I approached a young, college-educated woman at her Integra Telecom work station, extended my hand while her manager introduced us, and said, "It's nice to meet you, Claudia. I'm looking forward to spending the day working alongside you."

While Claudia graciously shook my hand, she clearly showed signs of apprehension. I don't blame her. After all, having the company's CEO/Mr. Boss Man/Head Honcho/Top Dog sitting next to you, watching your every move, asking stupid questions, and getting on your nerves hour after hour on this Wednesday, which would likely be the bumpiest and humpiest of Hump Days, was not something Claudia volunteered for. Nor would most (all, perhaps?) of her coworkers. She was probably thinking, *Why me? Oh my, oh my, why me?*

Little did each of us know that something transformative would emerge from our time together—although I certainly came to Salt Lake City with hopes that something significant would occur. I just didn't know if it would indeed manifest and what exactly that *it* would be. But I didn't have to wait long to find out.

But I'm getting ahead of myself a little bit here. Allow me to offer some context and some reflection on Chip Bergh and the whole notion of visionary guidance and how it fits into the Fusion Leadership model.

Chip demonstrated clear, focused vision in the two change-the-course leadership experiences that he told me about, which I conveyed in the previous pages. I've thought a lot about what he did, both in Singapore and in Boston. I won't pretend that the way my vision manifested at Integra Telecom can measure up to what Chip did. He transformed the multinational company Procter & Gamble, first turning a work culture on its head to succeed in significantly boosting P&G's Asian market and then shaking up a workforce after a multibillion-dollar merger to convert a historic old factory into a dynamic and productive work environment. But I do think the examples I'm about to share with you offer a different way to activate vision and energize an early-stage start-up business headquartered in the relatively sleepy northwestern corner of the United States.

Like Chip, I made it my mission to see my vision materialize.

Unlike Chip, who had an established business model he started from and then altered in important ways to achieve growth in market share, productivity, and profits, I didn't have an existing blueprint. But, as I've mentioned, I did know what would differentiate the young and ambitious Integra Telecom: We needed to reinvent the customer experience in data networking and communication. We intended to do this by providing customers a type of service they'd never seen before, make them want to do more business with us and deny offerings by our competitors.

And the key to it all, we decided, centered on the concept of locality.

At the time I cofounded Integra Telecom and started to shoulder my way into the über-competitive communications market, the giants of the industry—like Verizon and AT&T—employed a centralized service strategy, with large, monolithic call centers and huge, centralized provisioning operations. Even today, if you were to contact your cable company or your data company, you'd probably call an 800 number and talk to somebody in a different part of the world. You'd hear many conversations going on in the background, because the conventional wisdom and its accompanying strategy was, and still is for many companies, something like this: *If we centralize our customer service functions and streamline our operations, we'll achieve economies of scale and bolster our bottom line.* Blah, blah, blah.

Our retort to all that blah, blah, blah was a simple rejection: No, that's not the way to do things. This is a service business. It's not a widget manufacturing plant. At the end of the day what's going to create an experience for customers unlike anything they've had before with their communications provider is an actual human relationship, and the best place to cultivate a human relationship is at the local level. We wanted our employees to have their kids in the same schools as the kids of our customers. We wanted them to shop in the same stores, drive the same roads, and picnic in the same parks. We sought to build a local model, where consumers look their provider in the eye and have real, personal interaction and an authentic service relationship.

So that was the vision. Just like I'm sure Chip did, I put a lot of thought into how to energize hundreds of people to deliver on this model—not an easy task, given that many of these employees came out of the same big telecom companies that used centralized service models. I realized they might not find energy in this vision. I knew that I needed to create that buzz and get people fired up.

One way I went about it was to attempt to demonstrate the power of the local model through my own behavior, with the intent of inspiring others to deliver the message and communicate the vision. I made it a priority to spend a considerable amount of my days as CEO out in the field, in the offices where these local people were supporting our customers. So I would frequently travel and set up office next to the Integra Telecom employees who were serving customers. I saw the virtue of getting out of the proverbial ivory tower and sitting down with the frontline people.

Panning for Some Gold

That was the thinking that brought me to the Integra Telecom offices in Salt Lake City that day in the fall of 2002 to spend time with a provisioner. When the sales team brought in a new customer order, they would hand that order to the provisioner, who would essentially design the network circuit that would plug into that customer's location and turn on their data services. I called the manager of the provisioning group in Salt Lake City, a woman named Ellen, and told her I wanted to spend a day with one of the provisioners. I would sit at his or her workstation, in a chair next to him or her and help get customers up and running. Ellen said, "Great! Look forward to having you."

Of course, that provisioner was Claudia, and, as I've suggested, I'm sure Claudia's reaction to Ellen when she heard about my visit was anything but "Great!" Sensing Claudia's unease (or maybe *dread* is a more accurate characterization), I tried to disarm things a little. She had a stack of work orders on the corner of her desk, and I said, "Claudia, I want to be helpful. You know your job better than I do, and I hope that I won't be too much of a hindrance. I don't want you to just explain to me what happens here; I want to participate."

After a few awkward moments, we got to work; she walked me through the steps she would take, and I asked questions. Soon, we were enjoying each other's company—at least, I thought it was mutual.

One reason I came to Salt Lake was that I wanted everyone in the office to see the CEO sitting at the front line, taking a work order off the top of the pile, entering information into the provisioning system, and getting the customer turned on. Here's the service message I hoped I was delivering: *This is very important work. It's so important that I am here doing it, and it's important that it be done locally. I'm not at my home office, close to my family. I'm here with you because this is where our customers are.*

But I had another item on my agenda. I was looking for what I called "a golden nugget," something that would create an opportunity to make our model slightly better, something that would help elevate our service from a solid A to an A+. I prospected for these golden nuggets everywhere I traveled within the company. I suspected that Claudia probably had a few ideas. So as I was provisioning these orders, I was asking a lot of questions. I wanted to discover what might be frustrating for her, what would slow her down or cause her to take an additional step or make an unnecessary extra phone call to a customer. I hoped to find anything that would make the process of getting a customer activated a little easier, a little more reliable, and a little more user-friendly.

Sure enough, after a couple of hours, I stumbled across a golden nugget. Often, nothing would pan out on these missions, and I'd come up empty-handed, just like an unlucky gold prospector. In this case, though, I lucked out. What I learned was that this particular step in the process required Claudia to navigate between two different computer screens. We had one system that tracked all of our network locations and traffic routing. We had another that kept the records of our customers, such as their name, address, phone number, and other information. For Claudia to do this work, she had to toggle between these two different computer environments. It was quite inefficient. I could tell that slowed her down and frustrated her.

"Would it be easier," I asked her, "if this information that you got out of environment A were automatically populated in environment B?"

"Yes, that would be fantastic," Claudia said. "I can't tell you how much that would mean in terms of this entire process. It would really help provide better service."

Getting the IT People on It

So I took this golden nugget back to our chief information officer in Portland, who was responsible for all of our systems. I asked her, "Do you realize what we are doing to our people out there in Salt Lake City and in all our local service offices? We need to make this more efficient."

She agreed, and we immediately got our software gurus to reengineer the system. It wasn't a simple fix, but it was achievable, and we got that change implemented with the two systems interconnected.

I considered this a golden nugget for the obvious reason: It streamlined our customer service process in Salt Lake. But, equally important, if not more important, it gave me the opportunity to go back to Claudia and say, "Claudia, you have contributed something here. You helped make our model better. Because of you, workers are more efficient and customers are happier."

That became a bellwether moment, because for months and, really, years afterward, I know that Claudia would point to that and say, "I did that for this company that's now growing across eleven states. This was my contribution to the model."

The experience sent the message that our model thrives and

becomes better at the local level, next to the customer. Not only did this invigorate Claudia, Ellen, and everybody in their office, but it sent a very important message to our software engineers, chief information officer, and other employees in the Portland headquarters. Everybody in that ivory tower could see that we were a stronger company because of what happened out in Salt Lake City. In a sense, it shifted the center of gravity from Portland out to the local model. That shift accelerated the fusion process, creating a sense of shared commitment and shared ownership.

Ultimately, it also helped the vision take shape, which was the power of the close-to-the-customer local model. By going out in search of golden nuggets, I exercised a long-term, ongoing vision. What's more, I kept in regular contact with Ellen, and she became an evangelist for this type of model, not only for Integra Telecom, but for the other organizations she went on to work for. She brings that same passion to those she works with and the constituents she serves.

I must say it's a wonderful feeling to know that this simple little event had a truly profound and long-term impact on many people in terms of how they thought about the business. While the world of data communication might be quite boring to some people, it makes our world function. This little thing allowed Ellen, Claudia, me, and many others to conclude that we can make a difference. It mattered.

In this book, I've written a lot about the selfish-ego-versus-collective-ego struggle. The two egos definitely engaged in battle when it came to me traveling to spend time in the local Integra Telecom offices. I'd visit Salt Lake and the other offices about ten times a year. Now, the selfish ego—that narcissistic, sometimes lazy, always what's-in-this-for-me creature—would try to persuade me to go to Salt Lake City and other offices only once or twice a year, or not at all, and stay close to family and the cozy comforts of home. And sometimes, I'd succumb to the selfish ego and stay put in Portland.

But fortunately, the collective ego won its fair share of victories, because that part of me knew I needed to get on a plane and—well—get local.

I also faced other pressures to forgo spending time with the frontline people in distant offices. In 2002, at the time when I had that experience with Claudia and Ellen and their colleagues, we were all slogging our way through a recession. I had many tasks other than helping Claudia provision orders—important things that I could have been doing. For example, I could have been meeting with investors or dealing with strategic issues with my board of directors or any number of things. I think a traditional approach to leadership might conclude that spending those hours with Claudia was not the highest priority. But as a Fusion Leader, I would disagree with that, because the power of using that opportunity to demonstrate the model, to communicate the vision and the lasting impact it had, was much greater than spending four hours on the phone with an investor in New York.

Golden Nuggets as Nuclear Fuel

Like Chip Bergh, my veins flowed with ambition and expectations of high performance. These golden-nugget episodes encouraged a sense of shared commitment to the vision. I mined and polished many other nuggets across our thirty-three field service offices over many years, building a small army of committed field sergeants, like Claudia and Ellen in Salt Lake City, Janet in Minneapolis (the online training system discussed in chapter 1 was another golden nugget), and many, many others.

Yes, this tool, used to shift authority to the frontline workers, became central to the process of bringing our people together. But these golden nuggets also served as a form of nuclear fuel. Because our field personnel significantly influenced our operating model, I enjoyed enormous credibility in our other locations when it came to demanding results. And I set the bar very high!

Consider this motivational conversation that I regularly deployed when reviewing performance results with local management across our footprint. I would ask, "You have all the tools you need to deliver our unique service model, right?" Or "You have the processes and systems you need, correct?" Or maybe "You have the authority to handpick your team, right?" Then I would demand,

"Well then, with all these resources at your disposal, you should be able to beat the pants off of the competition, correct?"

I rarely encountered pushback on my demands for results, because the operating personnel who were in the crosshairs of my performance expectations were also joint architects in creating the business model. They were bought in. They were committed. They knew they were accountable. And I knew they would not let me down.

It worked amazingly well, catapulting Integra Telecom to the largest market share among our industry peers.

In short, this is the Fusion Leadership formula: First serve the collective ego to build a shared commitment, then, with the ultimate trust of your organization, set high standards and demand excellence in results.

Exerting Force to Exercise the Vision

Fusion Leadership served as my guide in shaping, manifesting, and communicating the vision of the local model. In the service businesses, it's all about people taking care of other people. That is achieved through relationships. While I think relationships can function electronically, I take the view that they work best when we can look one another in the eye, shake hands, or even wrap our arms around one another.

While I've stated a few times that the concept of nurturing a workplace environment where respect for all stands at the center of the fusion process, I don't want to give the impression that, as a leader, you don't have to exert your authority in a forceful way from time to time. You do—without being a tyrant, of course. I want to be very clear about this: Sometimes you absolutely must lay down the law, especially when it comes to something as critical as manifesting your vision.

Like most CEOs, I associated a lot with my management team, the C-level executives at headquarters, who were among the highest paid in the company. They had some of the bigger offices, were responsible for many employees, and worked in very stressful jobs with multiple demands. Because the industry had become accustomed to a centralized model, many of my executives felt that they were doing their job if they sat in their C-suites and issued mandates and dictated policy.

But I wanted them to live the local-is-best vision. In some cases, I found it extremely difficult to compel these executives to get out of their chairs, get on an airplane, and spend a couple days in the local offices. I felt if they didn't, their failure to do that would undermine what I had done with Claudia and Ellen in Salt Lake City and with other people in other locations. This was a priority of mine, and I felt it was necessary to articulate this vision—and not just through me and my actions but through all of the senior leaders at Integra Telecom. I can assure you: Some people hated it. They had families in Portland, nice roomy offices, and they also had a lot of work to do. They would resist it, and the resistance would come from people in a lot of different divisions of the company.

Consequently, I used a very direct tactic to try to compel people to get out of their chairs and into the local offices. Frequently, someone would schedule me to sit in on a meeting—we might be deciding the next technology to build or how to modify our billing system to be more competitive or whatever. I would often interrupt either at the beginning of the meeting or right when they were getting to the heart of the matter at hand. I'd ask them these sorts of questions: "Which customers have you talked to about this?" "Who in Minneapolis did you run this by?" Or "Which customer service representative did you get input from?"

They would often look at me with a blank expression on their faces, as if to say, *What are you talking about? I'm the senior vice president of this or that. This is my job. Why would I talk to those people?*

When I'd hear or sense pushback, I'd stop the meeting and say, "I'm not going to consider this decision any further until you can bring back to me the input from these people. We can look at PowerPoint all day long, but, until I have evidence that this is going to be embraced and used by people like Claudia in Salt Lake City, I'm not interested in talking about it anymore."

That drove people crazy. But it also drove home the point.

One person who was very instrumental in our growth was Fred, who ran our marketing group. Fred fully embraced the importance of locality in our business and management models. He's very smart, he's very good with people, and he got it immediately. Marketing, of course, is the brainstem of any competitive organization, and one of Fred's major roles was to own the product roadmap. What product should we be rolling out next year to stay ahead of the competition? If you don't get that right, you're going into the battlefield with one arm tied behind your back. It's critical to get products right.

Every time I would sit down with Fred for him to recommend something new, he would start by saying, "This idea came from such-and-such sales representative in Phoenix. He was in front of a customer who was having trouble. And this product has been designed to solve that problem. This customer needs this product." And he would give me the name of the customer service person who had been taking phone calls from customers with that same problem and how their lives would be easier if they had this particular additional feature in their service solution. Fred would always start the meeting with that perspective. Needless to say, this would delight me.

Fred ended up doing very well, rising to the top with a lot of promotions and increased compensation, and becoming one of a dozen of the most critical executives at the company. A lot of his success and skill, as well as his notable impact on the company, came as a result of his commitment to people and his willingness to get on an airplane, visit the branch offices, and support the local service model while demonstrating his dedication to it.

Over time, of course, organizations and behaviors change, and those people who didn't do as I asked or did it kicking and screaming the whole way either didn't stay with the company—by either their design or mine—or saw the light and got with the program. As the years went by, more and more people considered consulting far-flung coworkers and customers a valued behavior and began their presentations or their arguments with evidence that they had done their homework out in the field. Our culture evolved around that.

All of my strategic thinking and leading by example—with

lots of help from people like Fred, Claudia, Ellen, and many other adherents of this vision—paid off. Integra Telecom grew and prospered. We also revolutionized the way people thought about service models; rather than centralizing, we pushed operations out closer to the customer. And, while it makes sense talking about it now, that was a very uncommon approach at the time. I keep in touch with Ellen to this day, and when we talk, we often say, "Isn't it interesting that some of the biggest competitors in the world have moved parts of their organizations out of the ivory tower and into the field?" We would like to believe those moves were, in part, a competitive response to the success we had with our vision.

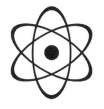

CHAPTER 7

WHOSE JOB IS IT TO STEP UP FOR THE CUSTOMER?

STEPPING UP FOR CHARLES: WALKING THE TALK BY HELPING STRANGERS PAYS OFF

On a beautiful sunny Saturday in northeast Portland, Oregon, my friend Dave Shaffer and his wife, Jean, attended a meeting to help attendees better understand the persistent societal problem of homelessness. Afterward, as they walked to their car—their minds packed with information, their hearts filled with empathy—they talked about what they'd learned, the importance of this societal problem, the knowledge and eloquence of the speakers, and the interest and compassion of the attendees.

The April 2010 gathering had been convened by the New City Initiative, a collaboration between the Ecumenical Ministries of Oregon and JOIN, a Portland-based nonprofit agency that works to end homelessness. And the meeting made its mark on the Shaffers.

"We left that day very impressed and deeply affected," said Dave Shaffer, who was, at that time, the CEO of DePaul Industries, a nonprofit organization that offers job opportunities to people with physical or mental disabilities by operating three outsourcing businesses in food packaging, temporary staffing, and security services. "Someone had asked a question: 'What are you supposed to do about all these panhandlers on the street? There's no easy answer. You just don't know who's scamming whom.'"

I couldn't agree more. I think many of us who sincerely want to help the poor ask the same legitimate question when we decide whether to dig into our wallet or purse and hand a homeless person some money.

The New City Initiative representatives and the audience reached a consensus on that question: If you have two dollars a day to help those on the street, you give a dollar to each of the first two people you see, and then you're done. If you have five dollars, you divide up your donations similarly. "And you shouldn't judge them," Shaffer said. "At a minimum, you should engage them as a person. Talk to them. Ask them their name. Begin some civil amount of dialogue."

Another message delivered that day resonated deeply with Shaffer: Often, the reason people are homeless is because they don't have relationships. Those who want to lend a hand need to reach out to the homeless and help them assimilate back into their communities. "Their relationships are broken down," he told me recently. "If they don't have a community, they're going to have trouble succeeding."

Little did Shaffer know then, as he and Jean drove home and continued to talk about the meeting, that within hours he'd come face-to-face with a challenging situation that would push him to make a difficult decision—one that would hold far-reaching ramifications for his organization, one with consequences that would reverberate among DePaul's management and rank-and-file employees alike. It presents a narrative that demonstrates a lot about Dave Shaffer as a person and as a successful CEO, how he embraced a common social challenge to place the collective ego ahead of his own selfish ego, and how his leadership style and strategy shaped and inspired DePaul's workforce.

Feeling like a "Second-Class Leader"

First, I think it's important to understand a little about Shaffer's evolution as a leader, DePaul's unique business model, its standing in the market, its mission to serve the underprivileged, and Shaffer's award-winning service to that model and mission.

Shaffer came out of college and followed a traditional yet fast-tracked financial career path, "going through the certified public accounting ranks fairly aggressively," he said. "I wanted to climb those ranks quickly, and, soon, I became the vice president of a company, fairly early on in my career. I didn't have a lot of mentors, so I managed people by what I learned from the textbooks I studied in college. I was a fairly autocratic, up-and-down hierarchical manager."

In 1997, after years of working in the business world, including a stifling and frustrating stint with a start-up gourmet chocolate company, Shaffer was reading the want ads one Saturday morning, looking for any new opportunity that might hasten a career change. He read one aloud to his wife that advertised an "entrepreneurial nonprofit" looking for an executive. It was, as you might have guessed, listed by DePaul (which had a different name at the time). Jean turned to her husband and said, "'Dave, that sounds like the perfect job for you,'" Shaffer recalled. "'You lead with your heart, and your brain follows,' she told me. And I'm glad she did, because that's always stuck with me."

The company's recruiters were impressed with Shaffer's resume—which he hand-delivered because he was so excited about this job prospect—and even more impressed with him. They hired him, and Shaffer worked diligently and, for the most part, happily as an executive in the C-suite at DePaul for a few years, hoping for a chance to become its CEO.

But something gnawed at him. "I came out of traditional for-profit businesses," he explained. "In the first half of my career here at DePaul, I felt, to a certain degree, like a second-class leader."

When he'd meet an executive in the for-profit community and talk about where he worked, that person would often say, with a hint of condescension, "Ohhhh, you're in the nonprofit sector. I see." That didn't sit right with Shaffer: "It bothered me even though I knew that DePaul was doing phenomenal work. I felt good about that, but in the business community, I didn't feel good about my career, my self-worth. I felt like my peers and those who I compared myself to were making more money than I was or were 'more successful' than I was. I wasn't the CEO then, but my ego and I thought I should be. I felt I was smarter and a better leader than my bosses, and that bothered me, too."

So he left the organization to reenter the for-profit business arena with a small commercial real estate firm. But, soon, DePaul came calling, wanting Shaffer to return. He was still wrestling with this internal struggle about the stigma that nonprofits somehow didn't measure up in perception and status to for-profit enterprises. But Jean spoke to him about how important nonprofits can be. His pastor counseled him as well. "He told me that if I used the same energies at DePaul that I had used in the for-profit arena, I could help make the world a better place," Shaffer said, adding that a few peers said that it must be rewarding doing the work that DePaul did. "Enough people hit me over the head with all of this, and I finally told myself, *This must be the place for me.*"

Changing Behavior, Making the Money

Shaffer came back to DePaul and was handed the reins of the company in 2007. As CEO, he transformed its business model by fully embracing—and, in fact, very vocally advocating—the mission of helping the disadvantaged while still maintaining a strategic and successful business approach.

"My predecessor never talked to our sales reps about the mission to help others," he told me. "The compensation was pretty good for the sales reps, and the motivation was *You can make a lot of money doing this.* That's how [his predecessor] inspired them—because the fear was that, if you start talking about disabilities, you'd be given an excuse to provide weaker service to our customers or to let sales numbers fall off. Or you'd turn into social workers because that feels good. So [his predecessor] never talked about the importance of employing people with disabilities."

Shaffer didn't like this at all. Consequently, one of the first things he did as CEO was to take a "macro approach," as he put it, to say to everyone: *Look, the more successful we are financially, the more people will be employed, and the more we can serve our mission.* "So, to our sales reps, I said, 'You guys are the biggest contributors in our efforts to get people with disabilities jobs. But you can do both of these two things: You can make money and take part in an inherently valuable and rewarding effort to help people in need. And that is much more powerful than just making money.'"

About ten people at the company came into Shaffer's office and told him that the organization's leadership had never talked about helping others before he took over. "I knew it, because I was there, and I was never comfortable with it," he said. "I also realized that my predecessor might have been right, and people would have turned into social workers and used excuses. But, ultimately, I didn't buy it, because I felt like the satisfaction of helping others is actually more of a motivator than money. And when you put the two together, you've got a pretty good mix."

Shaffer was right, and by talking at every opportunity about DePaul's worthy mission, he created other enthusiastic advocates within the organization, who, in turn, became more impassioned, praised the good work DePaul was doing, and, by extension, inspired others to do the same. The members of the organization became more committed to the cause. His strategic plan was very clear: As revenues go up, so too does employment for people with disabilities. These two goals—raise revenues and find people jobs—were "already aligned," Shaffer told me, "so why break them apart? But they had been separated, particularly for those people responsible for the revenue. I wanted to take advantage of that alignment, that integrated notion of mission and money. And that's why DePaul is so different."

It's also why DePaul grew so much with Shaffer at the helm. Consider this: A couple of years into Shaffer's tenure as CEO, DePaul was a regional player with offices across the Northwest. By 2013, it had grown to be one of the nation's largest employers of people with disabilities, generating $36 million in revenue and employing more than three thousand people, a sizable operation in this nonprofit sector.

These figures are important to Shaffer, but he really lights up when he talks about the numbers that have enhanced the mission. "Five years ago, the number of hours that were worked by people with disabilities was about 600,000 a year; this year, we should cross the million-hour mark," he said. "We're a national leader in this space."

Mind you, this growth occurred during the Great Recession. And that's even more impressive.

In the beginning, the challenge Shaffer struggled to answer for DePaul was how to drive the dual goals of advancing sales while also serving the disabled. Words were not enough. How could he get his colleagues to truly see the connection between helping people with disabilities and driving revenue growth?

Helping the Stranded, Complicating the Workplace

So let's get back to that April day in 2010 when Shaffer ran right into the face of a difficult decision. In the evening of the same Saturday that he and his wife participated in the meeting on homelessness, he, Jean, and their daughter Sarah attended a church service—it was the one-year anniversary of the death of Jean's father. On their drive home, they came upon an intersection in Southwest Portland with what appeared to be homeless people standing on three of the street corners—a young man in his twenties on one, a young woman on another, and an older man on yet another. The Shaffers noticed them and sped through the intersection, wanting to get back to a warm dinner in their comfortable home.

But within a block or two, the couple exchanged glances, and Shaffer turned his Honda Element compact SUV around.

"We looked at each other," Shaffer told me, "and said, 'Wait a minute. We can't do this [drive away and ignore the people in need]. What did we just do today?'"

Despite the potential danger inherent in an encounter with strangers clearly desperate for money and help, Shaffer and his family decided to reach out to these people. "We asked each other how much money we had, and in typical Shaffer style, we had only seven dollars in cash. I drove back and rolled down the window at the corner where the young woman was. I asked her, 'What's up?' She said in a deep southern accent, 'We're stranded. Our car blew up. We don't have any money. We have a little baby. And we're stranded.'"

The younger man, who was the father of the baby, came over to the car. "I asked him his name, and he told me it was Charles and his wife's name was Patricia," Shaffer said. "They told us more about their situation, that they were from Alabama, and pointed to the older man on the other side of the street, who was Charles's father."

Shaffer told the family he was sorry but that they only had seven dollars, gave them the money, and wrote down a phone number for Charles to call. It was the number for Paul, the organizer of the homelessness meeting. "'He can probably help you more than I can,'" Shaffer told the family. "'Try to reach him tonight, and if you can't, I would suggest you go to this church, which is my church, tomorrow. He'll be there.'"

The Shaffers went home, gathered up some food from their pantry, and returned to the intersection. But the family was gone. Shaffer remembered the name of the little motel where Charles said they had just enough money to stay. "It was a rough-and-tumble place with a glass-shielded entryway," Shaffer said. "We went to the front desk and asked about a young family from Alabama. The woman at the desk connected us with them. Soon, out of this motel room, walking across the parking lot, comes the family. We handed them the food, and they were very appreciative. They said they called Paul but couldn't reach him, so they were planning to go to the church tomorrow."

Shaffer also learned more about how they ended up where they were. Charles had been driving from Alabama, where he grew up and worked until he'd lost his job some months ago. He was en route to Seattle, where he and his father were to get a job on a salmon-fishing boat. But because of a few delays, they got to Seattle a day after the boat left the harbor. Charles thought he had enough money to drive back to Alabama, but somewhere a little south of Portland, his car's engine blew, and now he was looking for work.

"He kept saying to me, 'Dave, I really want to work. I'm a hard worker,'" Shaffer recalled. "My wheels started spinning right then and there and continued for much of the rest of the night. The next day, I met them at my church and told Charles to come to DePaul— that I might be able to get him a job."

That was a big step. By offering to help Charles even further than what he had already done, Shaffer was taking a chance. He was generating tension, on many levels, for him and his employees, setting into motion a series of actions and behaviors that resonated deep within the fabric of DePaul Industries.

"Shaffer Projects": Stressing the Staff

Let me provide some context here, because this was an unusual situation—not because Dave Shaffer was helping a poverty-stricken family; that's just like him, as he's a kind and generous person. But he told me that, while he didn't consciously think he was placing his own family in danger by approaching Charles and his family that evening, he did feel ill at ease. "I don't think I was all that worried about any danger," he said. "But I was uncomfortable. The fear was more about a social stigma. So breaking down personal barriers meant overcoming the social stigma."

What's more, by sticking his hand out further, bringing a person off the street and inviting him into his organization to apply for work, Shaffer was taking off his CEO hat and putting on the hat of one of his frontline workers. It's uncommon for a CEO to do that, to make it his job to personally step up for a customer.

Most importantly, Shaffer was essentially doing the work of his recruiters, and by recruiting Charles, he placed stress on his staff. "I was worried about the other people who worked at DePaul, those who reported to me or reported to someone who reported to me," he said. "I felt they would feel a tremendous amount of pressure to help Charles because I brought him in. Now, I told my staff, 'This guy is coming in, but he needs to go through the process like everyone else, and, if he fits and can work and can pass whatever he needs to, then I'd like to see him get a job. I think he can benefit from DePaul. But only if it works out.' Still, I'm sure they were thinking, 'Shaffer brought him in, and he needs preferential treatment.' That's the tension I was facing."

Shaffer also knew that the moment he told Charles to come to DePaul, he was making a commitment. He would be investing time, resources, and emotional energy. In his gut, though, Shaffer saw this as an important opportunity to change employee behavior by driving revenue growth through helping people. He saw an opportunity to fuse the organization together around his vision.

Charles applied for work, took a drug test, and failed—he liked to smoke pot—and had to clean out his system and retake the test. Shaffer and Jean got more involved with Charles and his family. "My wife wanted to help them in more ways than I did," he said. "One evening, about a week after Charles failed the drug test, Jean and I drove to their house out near Gresham [a Portland suburb]. She had packed up three bags of food. Charles was very embarrassed about failing the drug test but told me he'd be clean in a couple of days and would retake the test."

Shaffer acknowledged to me that he really didn't want to get this deeply involved and sacrifice as much as he did in attending to some of Charles's needs. "The first night that we were to drive out to Gresham, I knew the rush-hour traffic would be horrible, and I really didn't want to do it," he said. "So there was this conflict that it was infringing on my personal time."

But anyway, Charles retook the drug test, passed it, and got a manufacturing job that used his mechanical skills. A few weeks later, the Shaffers visited Charles and his family again, bringing more food—and Shaffer's investment grew. "Charles pulled me outside and said, 'Dave, I need a hundred bucks,'" Shaffer recalled. "'My car needs an alternator. The old alternator's on the kitchen table. I can fix the car myself. I'll pay you back next Friday.' I said, 'I'll give you the hundred dollars, but I only want fifty of it back. Call me when you get the car running.' This was on a Sunday night at 5:30 or so. Later that night, he called me and said he'd already gotten it running. The next Friday, there was an envelope in my mailbox with fifty dollars in it."

Eventually, Shaffer and Charles lost touch with each other—Charles had left his DePaul-generated job, asked for more money from Shaffer (who declined because he felt taken advantage of), and then faded out of Shaffer's life—but the impact of this relationship and Shaffer's decision to help Charles in the first place carried a lot of weight among DePaul employees. "Charles was very likeable, and he'd bring Patricia and their baby into the building from time to time. Everyone got to know him," Shaffer said. "Charles became representative of what DePaul is all about."

The Charles experience also served as only the first of Shaffer's recruiting efforts, because, over the next few years, he brought in five more people off the street who were seeking employment. Each of these people became known as a "Shaffer Project," a term coined by Travis, one of DePaul's vice presidents, to tease his boss.

Showing by Doing, Inspiring the Workforce

Initially, Shaffer helped Charles because he wanted to apply what he'd learned at the homelessness meeting and because—well—he truly wanted to help. It's in his nature. It also helped him personally reconnect with the organization's mission. "Subconsciously, I felt like I was removed from the hands-on involvement of people with disabilities," he said. "And this helped me reconnect."

But as time passed and he took on more "projects," his motives became increasingly strategic. He realized his behavior would likely be modeled, and that would promote a more passionate workforce. "I thought this would help people open their eyes, help them reexamine their jobs to see that one of the reasons they were working here was to help people," he said. "We all have this in us—the desire to help others—but sometimes we don't realize it. So this allowed people to say, 'It's okay to go the extra mile to help.'"

In my mind, another combination proves worthy of underscoring: Dave Shaffer's foray into frontline recruitment, combined with his upfront and vocal advocacy for the belief that mission equals money and vice versa, translated into successful, dynamic leadership that inspired those around him. And all of this advanced the collective good of the organization.

Shaffer's people did indeed model his behavior, and they became more closely drawn to him. "I saw in the employment specialists a closer relationship with them after I started recruiting [street people]," he said. "I told them, 'Look, if you can't get this done, it's okay.' I was very fair with them. Still, they knew that it was important to me. Therefore, it was important to them. The combination of filling a job as fast as they could for the revenue and the fact that they were positively affecting people's lives reinforced their commitment to our organization."

Hearing Shaffer tell the story of Charles brings forward a now familiar recipe in the Fusion Leadership model. Build mutual respect and shared commitment by serving the collective ego, then accelerate the vision and demand results. Shaffer's strategic decision to take on more "projects" clearly served as his tool to push his vision within the organization. DePaul's subsequent journey to become one of the nation's largest employers of the disabled provides evidence of his ability to insist on and achieve results from the organization as it grew committed to his vision.

And I'm certainly not the only one who recognizes this.

Dilemma: To Shun the Spotlight or Seek the Award

In 2012, Shaffer was nominated for the prestigious Ernst & Young Entrepreneur of the Year Award, in the Pacific Northwest, a nomination he'd also earned the previous year "when some other guy won it," he told me with a chuckle. (I had won the honor in 2011; he and I met when we were both nominees that year.)

Of course, nominees must tell the awards committee whether they accept or decline the nomination, and Shaffer had serious misgivings each year, especially in 2012. "I agreed to do it the second year after considerable consternation," he said. "I went through some trials and tribulations. I was concerned about calling attention to myself and diverting attention from where I thought it was more appropriate: DePaul and our efforts at addressing a social problem. It was uncomfortable for me."

It didn't help that a couple of DePaul board members made it clear to Shaffer that they weren't pleased he was accepting the nomination; they felt the limelight should be directed onto the organization, not the CEO.

And while a part of Shaffer—his selfish ego—was excited about the prospect of winning the award, he seriously considered declining the nomination, doing whatever he could to place public recognition on the organization, its people, and the mission, and going on with the day-to-day work of leading DePaul.

He needed counsel, and that meant turning to his chief advisor, his wife. "Jean told me that I had to do it," he explained. "She said, 'It's perfect for DePaul. And, you deserve this. You work hard.'" The president of his board also said, in so many words: "You have to do this. This is phenomenal." And his pastor told him, "This would be good for your organization. You should do it."

This struggle is indicative of Shaffer's Fusion Leadership style and the culture he had nurtured at DePaul, instinctively placing the collective ego at the top of his priorities. But he came to realize that if he won the award, the organization would reap internal and external benefits. Inside DePaul, it would validate that people who have disabilities can perform at the level the organization had been saying all along. "I understood that," Shaffer said, "and I also knew it would likely give everybody in the organization a morale boost: Yes, we're with a winner here. Everyone wants to work for a market leader, and we are a leader."

Externally, Shaffer felt it would add validation from a prospective customer perspective: "I thought that, on some level, customers would say, 'Wow, there's some truth in what these guys have been telling us. I'll listen to them when we're looking for some temporary staffing, because they have this all figured out.'"

Furthermore, the award would likely put to rest any lingering doubts Shaffer had about his self-worth, about being "a second-class leader" in a nonprofit setting as opposed to the for-profit corporate world. After all, other award winners included Jeff Bezos of

Amazon.com, Larry Page and Sergey Brin of Google, and Richard Schulze of Best Buy. As the process moved forward, Shaffer began to covet the award. He admitted to me, "If I was going to go through all this angst over the thing, I wanted to win it."

Well, sure enough, he won. And all of the external and internal benefits he thought would come to DePaul did—the morale boost, the validation of DePaul and its mission and model, and the stellar PR that reached potential customers and drove up business. "It gave us new energy. It gave us fuel to expand our model," Shaffer said.

It also provided a little levity around the office—at Shaffer's expense. His COO and other managers started calling him "Hollywood Dave" in front of employees and customers alike. "They'd joke about it but then come back and say, 'The award validates what we do,'" he said.

So Shaffer, Jean, and some of his management team members drove to Seattle to attend a gala awards ceremony in June 2012, where Shaffer would deliver his acceptance speech. That wasn't easy for him: "I didn't own a tux. It wasn't my style. It was a hard acceptance speech."

He used the opportunity to do a little staffing, telling the other winners and nominees that they needed to call him and hire people from DePaul. "I ask you to take a risk; that's what entrepreneurialism is all about: Hire people with disabilities," he told the audience that night. "The rewards will dwarf the risk ten times over."

A couple of touching encounters occurred that evening. "I had about a dozen people come up to me afterward to tell me that they had people with disabilities who were close to them," Shaffer said. "Although I didn't intend to, I had people crying at this event."

And then there was the reaction of one of DePaul's vice presidents, Travis, who'd coined the "Shaffer Project" term. He was known as a nice guy but also as a tough, no-nonsense former military man. "On the night of the ceremony," Shaffer recalled, "Travis pulled me off to the side and said, 'Look, this is validation of what this place has done and will continue to do, and you deserve this.' He never said that before. I knew he felt that way before then, but that was a special moment for Travis to get so personal. It meant a lot to me."

Ultimately, Shaffer said, that same sentiment rippled throughout the organization, promoting among the employees a renewed commitment to the cause. "I think all of us felt that the award was a validation that you could use business to do good. And you can do it on a big scale. Quite simply, we believe: This thing works."

SERVING FROM THE TOP: PROVIDING CUSTOMER SERVICE EVEN WHEN IT'S A PAIN IN THE . . . NECK

One of Integra Telecom's best customers, an engineer from a large technology company, had me cornered in my own office. And he wasn't happy. (That's an understatement.)

The day had started off well. It was a Thursday in early January of 1998, two years after I had signed Integra Telecom's incorporation documents. We had just installed the latest technology in telecommunications network equipment. It was a digital platform, brand new to the industry, and would deliver all sorts of benefits. My twenty employees and I knew that by having this technical advantage, we'd be able to compete and go toe-to-toe with the big telecom players. The multimillion-dollar investment was a big deal to us and our customers. And we wanted to celebrate.

So we scheduled an open house and invited our customers, because we were very proud of this new technology and what it would do for us and them. That Thursday was the day of the party. We spruced up the conference room in our headquarters on the west side of Portland, ordered wine and appetizers, and eagerly awaited that evening, when we could toast with our most important corporate customers and showcase this technology.

But then snow started falling. By midafternoon, we'd accumulated quite bit of it, which doesn't happen in Portland very often, and we wondered if we should cancel the shindig. Well, a lot of our customers in our early days were in business parks on the west side of Portland, and many of them were within walking distance of our offices. So we decided, what the heck, we'd open our doors—figuratively, because it was cold outside—uncork the wine, set out the food, and see who showed up.

As the workday came to a close and nightfall descended, we started welcoming our guests. Eventually, some thirty to thirty-five people from about a dozen companies were lifting their glasses to us and our new network equipment, with all its high-tech bells and whistles. We gave them tours of our facility, and, somehow, that's how I found myself in my office with a man I'll call Jason, the engineer from one of our largest customers, a brand-name NAS-DAQ-traded company with about two thousand employees. Initially, I was thinking, *How cool is this? We're a small start-up and we're serving this large public company, and its engineer is in my office wanting a sit-down face-to-face.*

Soon, I realized, however, that the positive feeling I had was fading as the discussion turned unpleasant. Jason had me right where he wanted—cornered, with no choice but to hear him rant about the problems he and his team were experiencing with our technology and customer service. He essentially ran down a list of issues. His company had recently moved into a new headquarters building, and we had activated service in that building for hundreds of people. But entire departments of people showed up to work one Monday morning only to discover that we'd messed up the installation. Vital information was not getting to the employees' desktops, or it was going to the wrong desktops. They were looking for a certain data speed that we thought we were delivering but we weren't.

So he was going through this litany of problems, and I was sitting there listening to him, wincing and worrying and saying to myself: *This is an unmitigated disaster. A real cluster-mess.* (Or words to that effect.) I thought, *Here I am, stuck in my office on this cold snowy evening with a guy who's getting more and more upset as he talks. Meanwhile, people in the other part of the building are laughing and*

drinking and eating very good food. This is one of our most import-
ant customers, and he's a very technical guy. I understand technol-
ogy, but I don't understand it well enough to be able to give him
good answers to his questions right now. If I screw this up, it could
really be a body blow to our company. And a refrain kept chiming
in my head, one that underscored the significance of this increasingly
contentious encounter: *They're one of our largest and best custom-*
ers . . . They're one of our largest and best customers . . . They're one
of our largest and best customers . . .

Panic began to set in as I wondered how I was going to appease
Jason.

"User-Friendly Service" — Mission On!

Now, let me step aside here before I finish this story to offer some
context. Whether you're somebody who's practicing Fusion Leadership or, really, any model of leadership, you need to address these
related questions: What makes your organization stand out? Why
does one company do something so much better than its competitors do? What's your mission? And how do you communicate the
organization's mission to your people? Most groups, be they companies, nonprofits, government agencies, colleges, or other insti-
tutions, write and try to adhere to a mission statement. Ideally, it
serves as the beacon that offers guidance during rocky times.

In the case of Dave Shaffer, as I described in the previous
pages, he wanted his salespeople and other employees to transcend the idea that they were working to make good money.
When he first arrived at DePaul Industries, he discovered that
many of the sales staff were only motivated by The Almighty Dollar. That drove him crazy. Yes, he knew that money's important,
but he wanted people to work for the organization because they
could also help people who are physically or mentally disabled
get employment. He felt that until the organization embraced that
underlying value, it wasn't the sort of company that he wanted to
work for and build. He wanted his employees to live the mission
of the organization, which was, and continues to be, to help the

disadvantaged. And Dave really drove that message home with his decision to take on the homeless Charles and his family, executing in a very tangible, real-life, street-level way the mission of DePaul Industries.

Now, Shaffer's story is different from mine, but as the leader of Integra Telecom, I knew we needed a mission, something that would differentiate us in the marketplace. And it became clear to me that our mission was to compete in the sometimes-cutthroat telecom industry by providing the very best customer experience. Our newly crafted and vetted mission statement reflected that: "To lead the competitive telecommunications industry in providing quality, user-friendly service."

Of course, it's not as magnanimous as helping the mentally and physically disabled with employment and turning their lives around. But that customer-service mission worked well for us. We felt that the users of telecom services were very frustrated with the status quo, in which if you have a service issue you have to phone some sort of call center where you sit on hold for too long and you have to explain who you are and why you're calling and what you buy from the company and then you get transferred to somebody else and maybe you get transferred again and then you call back the next day and reexplain it all over again. The big companies were almost—I wouldn't say indifferent—but they took this attitude: *Well, that's just the way it is. People are used to that kind of an experience. It's expected.*

So our mission, our vision, took a fresh approach toward serving customers. We not only wanted to meet the customers' needs; we wanted to delight them, as much as people can be delighted with a customer–company exchange. We thought that kind of experience would sell and that it would distinguish us in the marketplace. In fact, it ended up doing just that. This basic strategy enabled Integra Telecom to grow to be one of the ten largest landline companies in the country. But figuring out how to do that was a complicated matter. What does it mean to provide a differentiating experience? Is it exceptional friendliness on the phone? Is it having a bill that's easy to read? What does it mean?

That was one of the challenges that we wrestled with early on—defining what it was.

"Hello, Dudley? It's Jason . . . Again."

Consequently, as I sat there, trapped in my office that wintry night, taking a barrage of complaints from Jason, one thought kept rattling around my brain: What we stood for as a company was providing exceptional service, and we had really let this major customer down. I wasn't sure what to do.

And then, in a flash, something came to me. I got out my business card and wrote my cell phone number on it. I said, "Jason, do me a favor. Don't ever let yourself get to this level of agitation. If you see the smallest little thing, call me. I'm the CEO, and I will make sure that you don't get to this point ever again and that we take care of your needs." That got me off the hook for the time being, because I didn't have to respond immediately to his complicated questions. Besides, he could tell that I was over my head technically, and he was satisfied with taking my number.

It felt good to me, because, as the leader of the company, I could marshal resources. We had good technicians, and I was confident that we would take care of the company's problems. At that point, I felt like I had dodged a bullet, and he seemed accepting of my resolution. So we carried on, the evening wrapped up, and we all went home.

Well, the next day, I was back at the office, meeting with a number of people when my cell phone rang. I answered it and, you guessed it, it was Jason. He said, "You know, we've got this problem." And I said, "Okay, thank you for calling me." I asked him what the problem was, took some notes, made a call, and got somebody on it.

Later that afternoon, I was working at my desk, and Jason called again. I took notes and dispatched people out to solve his problem. Story over? Not even close.

For the next several weeks, Jason would call me two or three times a day. Let me repeat (in italics): *two or three times a day.* At that point in Integra Telecom's life, we were a growing company, and I had a lot of things to focus on. It seemed every time I'd dig into to a matter that required my complete attention, good old Jason would call. The calls were becoming a major source of annoyance and were really interfering with my ability to conduct business.

At the time, caller ID was a relatively new technology, but I had it, and I could see every time Jason's number popped up on my phone. I found myself wondering if I should let his call go to voicemail or not. After several days of interruptions, my selfish ego wanted to screen those calls. Not only did my selfish ego want to screen; it wanted to scream! There were definitely times when I second guessed my decision to give Jason my cell phone number. I had feelings of regret and worried that I wouldn't be able to do my job. I thought, *Wow, what have I done?*

And Jason would call at the most inopportune times. When I was under pressure to wrap up a meeting or respond to a board member or deal with a personnel matter, I'd hear that customized cell phone ring, see the caller ID number, and know that I was about to get an earful of Jason's problems. That voice inside my head would tell me that taking a customer's calls wasn't technically my job. I wasn't a technician, and I wasn't a customer service person. I was the CEO, damn it!

But ultimately, I understood that I had to drop what I was doing, pick up the call, and say as nicely as I could, "Hi, Jason. How are you?" The organization's collective ego whispered in my ear, *Grin and bear it. Remember what this company stands for. If Integra Telecom is really going to compete in this market, you've got to take this call. You gave this guy your word, your assurance that you would make things right.*

Often, when Jason would call, I was in meeting rooms with other people, and they would see me interrupt what we were doing to deal with a customer issue. So my attention to those calls resonated within the organization. I felt that if we really were going to provide a different service experience, one of the things that would set us apart would be that the CEO was willing to drop everything to take care of a customer. If the CEO does that, then it wouldn't be unreasonable to expect the CFO to do that or the COO or the manager of customer service or anybody else at Integra Telecom. So I resolved myself—as inconvenient as it was and as tempting as it was to become exasperated over it all and ask Jason to call someone else who could help him directly—to just deal with it.

That resolve paid off, because after a couple of weeks, Jason stopped calling. We got every problem fixed and every issue resolved, and Jason was not only satisfied, but he eventually became positively evangelical toward singing Integra Telecom's praises. I couldn't begin to count the number of technology companies we won because he would offer a glowing referral about us to his other technology friends. He ultimately turned into a very strong advocate for us. Years later, we would serve a significant percentage of the technology companies in our territory, and I really think we secured much of that market because of what happened when and after Jason cornered me during that open house. He stood behind us and described to others why we were different and better than our competitors in the marketplace.

I used to recount that story years later, when we grew to be a very large company. Sometimes, at employee meetings, I would tell it to try to rally the troops. It was a powerful story, because people would hear me describe that and they would think, *Gosh, if the CEO is willing to do this, maybe I should be willing to do it as well.* The story became well known and really helped deliver our message. And it wasn't just well known because I talked about it. Jason did too. It served as a way to bring life to the mission statement that hung on the wall. And the story gained in relevance as we matured into eleven states, with thirty-three local service offices, all close to the customer, just as I stayed close to Jason during his network challenges.

I was happy to hear how Dave Shaffer brought life to his mission of moving people away from just working for money and encouraging them to work for the fulfillment of helping people who are disabled get jobs. Now, what I did was not nearly as socially redeeming as what Shaffer's company did, of course, but it did motivate the workforce to serve other people politely, expediently, enthusiastically, and effectively.

ON HANDS AND KNEES

When you lead with the Fusion Leadership model as a template, you occasionally find its principles guiding you in the most unlikely of situations, when you least expect it. Sometimes by applying Fusion Leadership you motivate others. And other times, you motivate yourself, and maybe discover your swagger.

Take, for example, an encounter I experienced in a dry cleaner shop on a drizzly Tuesday morning in the late winter of 2007. By this time, Integra Telecom had grown considerably, with accounts from many of the large technology companies, thanks in part to Jason's referrals, and employed more than two thousand people. But we still served businesses of all sizes, including Peacock Cleaners, in Southwest Portland, which was run by a very nice, hard-working woman named Ruby. On a spectrum of significant big-dollar customers, Peacock Cleaners was positioned on the opposite end from Jason's tech company. We probably charged his firm $10,000 a month at that time for the services we provided. I'm guessing that, with Peacock's two phone lines, Ruby probably paid us about $150 a month.

On this chilly wet morning, I stopped at Peacock to drop off a load of dirty laundry and pick up a stack of cleaned clothes. I parked my car, rushed through the raindrops, opened the door, greeted Ruby, and chatted with her as she retrieved my clothes from the conveyor. I was the only customer in the shop until someone else came in as I was about to pay. Ruby swiped my debit card, but the card machine didn't register it. She swiped the card a couple more times, and it became obvious that the thing wasn't going to work. And then another customer walked in, so a bit of a line was forming behind me. The other customers were waiting for the transaction to go through, and I felt the tension level in the room rising. People wanted to pick up or drop off their clothes and get to work.

Then I thought, *Okay, this may not be her machine. It could be her phone line. If it's her phone line, it's likely something I'm some-what responsible for.* Now, I don't think Ruby knew I was the CEO of the company—at least, she didn't indicate that she knew. Nor did she look at me at all for help. She looked at me as a customer.

So I was standing there, thinking to myself, *I have a choice to make. I can just continue my identity as a customer in line, wait-ing for this technology to get resolved, or I can take on the role of being an employee of this organization whose mission is to dis-tinguish itself on the customer experience, and help her.* I suffered through this mental back-and-forth tug-of-war. I was in a hurry and wasn't in the mood to engage a relatively minor customer. I had important matters to attend to. People needed me on the job, at the helm. I was trying to convince myself to continue acting my role as just a regular guy at the front of the line waiting for this thing to get fixed.

Ruby kept struggling with the machine, and I started challeng-ing my decision to stay undercover, so to speak. Since the experi-ence with Jason and the technology company, many years had gone by, and we'd evolved into one of the hottest growth companies in the United States. I was feeling pretty good about myself in my role as Integra Telecom's leader, but, right then, I thought, *You know, if I'm really going to stand behind what this company is about, I've got to help Ruby out.*

I put my dry cleaning back on the rack and said, "Hey, can I give you a hand?" I started crawling around the counter, tracking wires and checking, first of all, to see if the machine was plugged in to the phone jack. It was, so then I began doing some basic diagnos-tic stuff. I saw Ruby's normal telephone and realized that, if it had a dial tone, then the odds were high that the card machine might be the problem. I checked the dial tone. Nothing. I unplugged the cords and plugged them back in, spending another five minutes crawling around the counter on my hands and knees. During that time, she figured out that she could still run her business by tak-ing the customers' dirty clothes and giving them their clean clothes and simply writing down the amount customers owed. She also wrote down their credit card information so she could process the payments later. That seemed to satisfy everybody in line. So she was taking care of business while I was scrambling around the counter trying to figure out why her two phone lines were dead.

I wasn't able to get them working, but I did figure out that nothing in the store was causing the problem. So I grabbed my cell phone and called our service center. I told them where I was and that there was a problem with the connectivity to the network. I essentially got our service department on top of the situation.

By that time, Ruby had cleared up the line of customers, and things had settled down quite a bit. I handed her my business card and told her to give me a call if the problem wasn't fixed within an hour or two. "Please let me know, Ruby," I said. I grabbed my clothes and rushed back to my car.

I didn't hear anything from Ruby until I went back in there the next time I had a pile of dirty clothes. When I saw her, she was the kindest, sweetest, most grateful person. I had made a friend for life. She reported that our service department had fixed the problem within an hour. "I wouldn't have known who to call or exactly what to tell them," she said. "So thank you so much for helping me get through that." She was just delighted and told me that after she looked at my card and saw I was Integra Telecom's CEO, she couldn't imagine that the presidents of Verizon or AT&T would ever consider crawling around on hands and knees and helping her get the problem fixed. And, frankly, I don't . . . well, let me just leave it at that.

Ruby Tuesday

Until now, I hadn't told that story to more than one or two people. That is, because I didn't make a big deal out of what transpired with Ruby on that rainy Tuesday, I didn't choose to use the event as a fusion tool, where my actions reverberated out to others. Maybe I should have made more of it, but, by that time, our mission was well established; the organization was performing at a high level, and I was confident in the degree of organizational trust and shared commitment we enjoyed. We had hit the market successfully, reaping sizeable profits, expanding our market share, and getting written up in a lot of papers and industry journals. There wasn't any doubt about what we were doing, that we were acting on our mission to lead the industry in customer service.

But I tell the story now because I was the one with doubts. Initially, I was unsure about what to do that day—a day I think of as "Ruby Tuesday," invoking a Rolling Stones song to help me better remember the exchange. In some small but important measure, it acted as a test and raised questions about my character. Had I become consumed with self-importance? Had I grown to a point where I was above crawling on my hands and knees to help someone? Had I become the stuffy CEO who could have easily just walked out and not worried about any repercussions regarding a $150-a-month customer? The value I got out of that seemingly simple experience was that it served as my own reminder of the incredible impact that occurred with Jason seven years earlier. While Ruby Tuesday didn't create a great ripple effect, because I basically kept it to myself, nor did it generate referrals for new business, it did redouble the strength of my own conviction that not only is Fusion Leadership a successful model to activate, but it's fun too. I made a friend that morning. I became a geek version of a hero to a small business.

Deep down, I knew it would have been difficult to reconcile the opposite decision—refusing to help Ruby—with myself. Once again, the incident adds substance to the view that all human behavior is ultimately self-serving, even if others benefit from that behavior. At the time, I thought, *If I continue to play the role of just another Peacock customer and walk out of here without helping Ruby, how can I return to the office, look people in the eye, and expect them to deliver on the service model that's been so successful for us? Have I really become more important than the fundamental model of the company?* That thought was ultimately the clincher that convinced me.

More importantly, my redoubled enthusiasm for our service model drove my expectations for Integra Telecom's performance even higher. That year, we went on to achieve great things, being featured in a national publication as "A Study in the High Touch

Approach" to customer service. The satisfaction and significance I derived from Ruby Tuesday drove my confidence in demanding excellence from our operations and every single employee. I knew, from fresh experience, that we were better than our competitors. I knew that I had the support of our entire workforce, and I was exceedingly confident in setting the performance bar even higher.

Ruby Tuesday inspired a certain swagger in my competitive confidence, and I believe that the industry accolades we received inspired a competitive swagger in our entire organization. We had become the winning team. The fusion process was now years into its organizational impact, and the company was performing at its highest level.

Thank goodness I acted as I did on that rainy morning, because the experience turned out to be the foundation for what became a very gratifying relationship. Ruby and I are friends. I was able to create that friendship because I extended myself to help somebody else. I hope I'll never be too big for that.

CHAPTER 8

WHO IS GOING
TO KICK ASS—AND HOW?

FLEXING LEADERSHIP MUSCLES:
THE TRAIN IS LEAVING THE STATION
AND YOU HAVE A CHOICE TO MAKE

On a Thursday in 1995, Ray Davis, CEO of Umpqua Bank, in the small town of Roseberg, Oregon, asked his assistant to call a meeting of the financial institution's officers for 6:00 that evening, which meant there'd be a gap between the time the bank closed at 5:00 and the start of the meeting. That was a strategic move by Davis. "I wanted them to be inconvenienced," he told me. He deployed intentional inconvenience.

Surprised, his assistant asked, "What's it about?"

"I don't completely know yet," he said. "But when I get there, I'll have it figured it out." He knew that some of the officers would balk at attending, wanting instead to go home for dinner or out for the evening, but he told his assistant to tell them, "I strongly advise them to be there."

Davis booked a meeting room at a local Roseberg motel, because the small community bank didn't have a conference room and the motel would be an unfamiliar—and, yes, inconvenient—setting for the Umpqua bank officers. Davis liked that he found an offsite, out-of-the-comfort-zone location to convey an important message: He wanted change, and he wanted everyone onboard. And at that meeting, he decided to take a risky approach to deliver the news.

At the time, Davis had only been leading Umpqua Bank for a little over a year, leaving Atlanta, Georgia, and his job as the CEO of a bank consulting firm to take the reins of what was then a "sleepy little bank," as he called it, founded sixty years earlier by some lumberjacks who wanted to create a bank to cash paychecks. Umpqua (then called South Umpqua State Bank) had five branches and forty employees. When he first learned about the job, Davis had to get out a map of Oregon to find out that Roseberg is in the southern part of the state, surrounded by forests. "I didn't know where the hell it was," he recalled.

While considering the possible new position, Davis knew that if he accepted the job, he'd end up turning the bank on its head—not immediately but eventually. And he let the Umpqua board members know that right up front. "I told the board—and they were drug-store and hardware store owners, farmers and lumber guys, salt-of-the-earth people, good people—I told them, 'If I come out here, everything you know about banking is going to change,'" he said. "'We're talking about significant turmoil, and people are going to be upset. Some will be your friends who have worked at the bank for twenty years, and they'll call you at home and complain about me and the changes I'm making. But we're going to create value. And if you're up to it, that's great. If not, no hard feelings, but I'm not the guy to hire.'"

The board hired him.

During the first few months on the job, Davis watched, learned, and assessed. "I didn't want to come out here and start changing the world in two weeks," he said. "That would have been a hor-rible mistake." Davis intuitively knew he needed time to earn the confidence and respect of his team so they would follow his lead. He needed to solidify his vision and draw the organization together.

"So, after a number of months," he continued, "it became pretty clear that, if we were going to create or improve the intrinsic value of the company and for our shareholders, then we were going to have to make some significant changes. The question I really was asking myself at the time was, *Why would anybody bank with us?*"

With some large national chain banks in the area, including Wells Fargo and Bank of America, Davis knew that Umpqua couldn't "out-resource them, out-computer them, or out-product them," as he put it. Competitors could beat the community bank anytime they wanted in these areas. "But we could out-deliver them, because we're agile, small, quick; we can dodge and weave," he said.

It seems Davis and his managerial team could also out-innovate the national players. They embarked on the creation of a delivery system that was uniquely different. They called in high-quality consultants to help redesign the look of the Roseberg branch and turn it into what they called a "store." Davis wanted employees to start referring to Umpqua as the "World's Greatest Bank." As part of a crisp new rebranding campaign, he recommended a change in the name of the bank. "Why was *state* in the name?" he asked. "Why *south*?" He had plans to hire hospitality experts to extensively train, and retrain, bank employees. He wanted to grow the business and expand to new markets.

Many of the Umpqua employees liked the way their CEO was transforming their branches. But some wanted the change to occur incrementally. And a few wanted no such change. To this day, Davis doesn't remember exactly what he saw or heard that he didn't like that prompted the call for a spur-of-the-moment meeting during that time in 1995. "Something that I wanted to happen didn't happen—I don't remember what it was—but I was frustrated that things were not happening fast enough," he said.

Better to Show Intensity than Tell It

So, shortly after 6:00 in that Roseberg motel meeting room—with about two dozen top Umpqua employees crowded in, a sense of unease lingering and voices murmuring—Davis steeled himself to march in to address his troops.

Now, it's important to note that Ray Davis, a friend of mine, is certainly a man who's ambitious and driven. But he's also friendly, outgoing, and helpful. He likes to be liked, but he prefers to be respected when it comes to his workforce. He works hard to get to know his employees and strives to find ways to support them whenever and however he can. In fact, he refers to himself not as the bank's CEO but as its HoS, *head of support*. "My job," he often tells people, "is defined as making my frontline employees successful. My role is to support them in that success."

But he wasn't about to play the nice guy at that meeting. He knew he had to become a chameleon, so to speak, to get into character and take on a different role. "I needed to get a little angry," he recalled. "In other words, it's like a fighter going into a ring: 'Okay, give me just a minute. Deep breath. Okay, I'm ready to go now!'"

Ready indeed. Davis purposely waited until all of the bank managers and department heads had arrived before he entered the meeting. He took that deep breath and figuratively shadowed-boxed a little outside the room before strutting into the center of the ring. "I went in, and I leveled 'em," he told me, smiling. "I basically said to these people, 'You all know what I want to get done. You know how fast we want to get there. But some of you haven't bought in. So let me just say this to you: At 5:05 tomorrow evening, at the end of this work week, the train is pulling out of the depot. Get on it. If you don't, you've got a problem.'"

And then Davis walked out. He didn't look around the room to survey the crowd. He didn't wait for questions. He simply walked out as briskly as he'd walked in, letting the stunned Umpqua officers sit there, wondering what just hit them. His plan was carefully considered, his strategy crystal clear. "The purpose at that time," he recalled, "was for these people to *see* the intensity. Not hear about it. I wanted them to see it because I'm a believer in *Tell me, and yeah, I get 80 percent of it, or maybe 50 percent of it. But show it to me and I'm in. I know what you want.* . . . So I showed it to them."

What Davis did that day demonstrates another way a Fusion Leader operates. That is, he or she must defend the vision *and* the collective ego, at all costs, no matter what it takes. His out-of-character posture served as a tool to push his organization forward and motivate his employees. Sometimes a Fusion Leader must transform him- or herself into a different person. In Davis's case, he took on a boxer's persona before stepping into the figurative ring to deliver his blows—and that was risky, especially given that he was relatively new to the company. He had to be egocentric on behalf of the organization—*this is what I want, and I want it now*—strut into the meeting room, lay down the law, and act a little like a dictator, certainly not like a man who wanted to make friends. And he was somewhat vulnerable in doing that.

It sounds like a paradox, but by showing his managers and department heads that he was—or, at least, could be—an egocentric, autocratic ruler, which is not the way he generally relates to people, he became vulnerable. After all, he could've come across as a bossy blowhard, ruining the fusion process he'd been cultivating for the year-plus of his tenure at Umpqua. His bold act certainly surprised everyone in the room who was not named Ray Davis, and many people don't like surprises—at least, not one like this. As with the other examples of leadership articulated in this book, Davis sublimated his selfish ego for the long-range collective ego.

Generating Big-Time Results

So here's the important question: Was that "shotgun blast," as Davis has called it, effective or merely a simulated manifestation of unleashed corporate temper? That is, how did those bank officers respond to Davis's tactic?

Well, it turns out, they reacted even better than Davis had expected. Several of the bank officers came to work the next day with renewed passion for their jobs; Davis saw this in their eyes and, more importantly, in their performance. "They got pretty fired up," he said. A few came by his office to say, "Ray, that was exactly what we needed. Thanks." And two or three decided that they weren't ready for the changes Davis was putting into place. "There were a few twenty-five-year veterans that essentially said, 'I don't want to do this. It's time to go.' And, frankly, that was great," he recalled and chuckled.

But the vast majority of the officers boarded that 5:05 train, and the Umpqua Bank Express took off, full steam ahead. In the nearly two decades since that meeting, Umpqua has, in many ways, led the industry in customer-centric innovation, opening many new stylish stores that feature a sense of pizzazz and offer enticing perks like free chocolate coins and coffee, events and book readings, and even yoga classes. Inside, the sleek, well-designed stores look more like "hotel lobbies than traditional bank branches," according to reporter Mary Wisniewski in an article in *American Banker*. What's more, Umpqua's customer base kept growing, and Davis made sure the bank kept expanding.

In 2014, Umpqua's holding corporation acquired Sterling Financial Corporation in a transaction that was valued at about $2 billion. The merger created the West Coast's largest community bank, with approximately $22 billion in assets, five thousand employees, and 394 stores across five states—Oregon, Washington, Nevada, California, and Idaho. The combined company also established a $10-million community foundation to help people in their communities who needed assistance.

Talk about results!

While Davis can't completely credit his decision to issue a firm challenge to his bank officers at that meeting as the main reason for Umpqua's success, he does believe it was pivotal in getting buy-in from his employees. "I think, in terms of the growth of our company, it's one of those 'aha' moments that people remember," Davis said, adding that, from time to time, he makes reference to that meeting, using his train analogy, which has become a part of company lore. "A few times, I've said, 'Maybe the 5:05 needs to pull back into the station and pick up a few more people.' The old-timers who were there, and even some people who've only heard about that meeting, know exactly what 5:05 means, and they smile when I refer to it."

Actually, Umpqua employees smile often on the job; they're generally happy, and that's reflected in the frequency with which the bank and its many stores have scored high in best-places-to-work rankings. That job satisfaction starts at the top, with Davis. Despite earning many individual accolades through the years, including being named by *US Banker* as one of the twenty-five most influential people in the financial industry in 2005, he said he takes greater pride in cultivating relationships with his employees. "I would say that one of the things I'm most proud of is my working relationships with the associates of the company. I like them, and I think they like me—pretty much most of the time," he added, as he and I both laughed. "But I do enjoy that. I like being around people who motivate and inspire me, and as a group, they do that."

A Phone Call that Really Mattered

Umpqua employees also know that Davis genuinely cares about them. Consider this. One of the innovations that Davis implemented, which has now become one of the bank's many trademarks, is the in-store red phone that customers can pick up to call the CEO directly. During a program in which Umpqua employees received customer-service training from hospitality experts with the Ritz-Carlton Hotel chain, Davis came up with the phone idea. "Out of that [training] process," he recalled, "it dawned on me: We're a small community bank, why not have people call me? So I decided we should put phones in all of our stores."

He gets four or five calls each month, frequently from people who just want to know if the CEO is really at the other end of the line. "When people call and hear me say, 'This is Ray Davis of the World's Greatest Bank. How can I help you?' there's often silence," he told me. "And then they say, 'Is this really Ray Davis?' And I say, 'Yes it is. What can I do for you?' They say, 'Nothing, I just wanted to see if you'd pick up the phone. Good-bye.' But I think it makes a lasting impression on those people."

Well, one of the frequent callers was, shall we say, an unusual customer, who would call Davis from an Umpqua store in Seattle every few months or so and spew non sequiturs into the phone. The first time this woman called, Davis recognized immediately that she was mentally unstable—not a difficult assessment given that she launched into a rant that included this charge: "The streetcar's not doing it. Why'd you paint it blue?" When he asked, "May I ask you a question?" she said, "No, you can't."

Davis thought of ways of getting off the phone as politely as possible as the woman's voice began to rise to a yell. Simultaneously, he worried about the employees in the Seattle store. Finally, he wished the woman "a great day," said goodbye, and hung up. He then immediately called the store manager, who he imagined felt horrible about the incident and might even be in a difficult— perhaps dangerous—situation.

I asked my friend if, at that time, he wished he hadn't started the phone line. He said, "No, not at all. I knew that that store manager was probably sick about the call and worrying that I was put out. So I called the store and said, 'So tell me, are you guys okay?' The manager said, 'Oh, Ray, we're sorry.' I said, 'No, no, don't be sorry. That's okay. You have anybody call me that you want to call, and don't worry about that. I just want to make sure you guys are all right. And if somebody does come into your store who really is disruptive, don't hesitate to call the police. I mean, they need help. They're not necessarily bad people. They just need help. We understand that. She's okay. She's just not playing with a full deck. So no, that doesn't bother me.'"

Notice what Davis did there. He flipped the circumstances with the second phone call, the one he placed, the one that really mattered. He transformed a situation from being an annoying, maybe even disturbing, incident that disrupted his day into something that the bank manager benefited from because he took the time to call her, inquire about the employees' safety, reassure them that he wasn't upset, and allowed them to feel important, in a sense. But, first and foremost, his return call demonstrated that he cares about them—and that's what relationship building is all about.

It's also an example of what a Fusion Leader does, because, importantly, it's the right thing to do, but also because it makes good business sense, whether Davis consciously recognized it at the time or not. That is, you can bet the ranch that his call to the manager rippled out to other employees and, eventually, to other stores throughout the organization. In fact, I asked Davis if the manager told others and essentially became an evangelist of the culture. "I guarantee she did," he said. "That's why it's so important for people to understand the impact they have on others." A simple gesture like this, and the subsequent positive chain reaction, builds trust and motivates the workforce: If the CEO looks out for his employees, the employees tend to look out for one another—and for their customers.

FIRING AN EMPLOYEE, SUPPORTING THE TROOPS

Sometimes, defending the collective ego means getting rid of one of your employees. At times, you move as swiftly as a blade dropping in a guillotine. I can't recall, however, a time that compares with the urgency Ray Davis undertook in the example he shared with me.

Years ago, Davis had hired a very bright guy we'll call Mike, who, within the first week on the job at Umpqua, was making off-color remarks to some of the female employees. Davis got wind of it and called Mike immediately. "I said, 'Hey, Mike, what's this? What are you doing? Don't do that,'" Davis recalled. "He apologized and said he wouldn't do it again."

Davis felt confident he had fixed the problem. But then, some time later, he and his wife were vacationing in Washington, DC. He came back to his hotel one day and saw the phone's red light blinking. He listened to the message, and it was Julie, his assistant, who said, "Ray, call as soon as you get the chance. We have a problem we need to talk to you about." He had three other messages on the machine. "So," he said, "the second call was, 'Ray, this is Julie. I called about forty-five minutes ago. You really do need to call as soon as you can. We have a problem.' By the fourth call, she was like, 'Ray, where in the hell are you?! You gotta call in here!'"

Davis called, and Julie told him that Mike had been terrorizing people. She told him that half of the accounting people were going to walk out. They were all crying. It was a disaster. Mike wasn't making off-color remarks—he'd gotten over that—but he was raging and acting as tyrannical as the famous Soup Nazi on the *Seinfeld* TV show, ordering people around and screaming at and heaping abuse on them. Davis immediately recognized the threat that Mike presented to the organization and the fusion process. Davis wasn't scheduled to fly back to Oregon for a few days, but he cut his vacation short and asked Julie to book him a flight for the next day.

Davis vividly remembers the following day, when he visited the Umpqua branch where Mike worked. Davis told me, "I remember going into the office—and one of the rules that I have in my company is that, when we have casual days like Friday, you can come in casual, but you can't wear jeans into our bank. If you work for us, no jeans. I don't want to see that. But that day, I had jeans on, and I walked right upstairs to the executive offices and Julie. I didn't say hello to anybody. I said to her, 'Julie, where's Mike?'"

She told Davis he was in a meeting with a large, well-known public accounting firm in a nearby conference room.

"'Great,' I said. I opened up the door, and there he was.

"I said, 'Mike, can I see you?'

"'No, we're in a meeting,' he said.

"'I need to see you,' I told him.

"He must have been thinking, *What's this? Ray's not due back yet. And what's he doing in jeans?*

"I walked him to my office, and I said, 'You're fired, and I want your ass out of this bank *now*!'

"And he started to say, 'Oh, this is about . . . '

"I said, 'Yeah, we're not going to talk about it. You're done. I want you out.'

"'Well, let me go get my stuff.'

"'No, get out now. I will make arrangements to have someone call you and meet you back here after everybody's gone so you can get all your stuff out without causing a scene.'"

Davis told me that it was a brutal encounter, an extreme case. "Boy, it was," he said. "I mean, he was out of there. And I went in to the accounting guys and said, 'Meeting's canceled.'"

Davis didn't need to hear Mike's side of the story, because he had enough confidence in Julie to know that all that she'd said was true. "I was not going to go in and have him try to explain it away," he said. "That would have been a waste of my time. It happened. I knew it happened. If he wanted to make a big deal out of it afterward, fine."

He told Julie that he'd fired Mike and that he needed to go home but asked her to tell the accounting people he'd meet with them first thing in the morning. The next day, when the CEO walked into the office, wearing a business suit instead of Levi's, his employees, who had gotten wind that Mike was gone, greeted him with loud applause and a standing ovation.

Davis smiled a lot when he told me the story—not because he likes such tumultuous encounters, of course, but because he's proud of his decisive action, his leadership. And because his people recognized that their boss had their backs.

It's safe to say that the story—Mike's swift dismissal on a day Ray Davis was supposed to still be on vacation with his wife, enjoying our nation's capital, Davis wearing jeans and canceling the meeting with people from the Big Five accounting firm, and the standing O he received the next day—spread throughout the organization like a viral YouTube video.

Wish Program Changes Lives, Benefits Bank

When you talk with Ray Davis, the word *empowerment* comes up a lot. He told me that he and his leadership team find ways to empower their employees and tell them, "Now go change people's lives." One of the most significant ways Umpqua does this is through its Wish upon a Star program, which really carries an impact on people by investing in the stores' communities. In this program, which Davis initiated, the bank sets aside money and grants wishes to customers in the bank or people in the community. It runs the ten days leading up to Christmas, so each market that participates in the program grants ten wishes.

For example, a young mother in southern Oregon grew up with chronic dental problems. She had missing teeth and a horrible self-image. She was intelligent and making a contribution to the community. But because of her low self-esteem, she was holding herself back.

The program allows the local Umpqua associates to review Wish upon a Star submissions and select applicants—sometimes they're individuals, and sometimes they're organizations—to receive the funding; often, it's a big chunk of money. So in this southern Oregon town, the Umpqua employees picked this deserving woman. She was able to receive badly needed dental work, and it enhanced her quality of life enormously.

Now, naturally, this isn't just a philanthropic endeavor, as Umpqua gets a lot out of the program from a business perspective. The benefits are threefold: 1. It provides tangible evidence that Umpqua is a community bank and invests in its community and shows that the bank values its customers and is willing to go above and beyond on behalf of a customer. 2. It empowers the frontline associates to be participants in their communities by improving people's lives. 3. It creates enormous goodwill for the bank. In short, it's a powerful tool.

On occasion, Davis will choose a winning recipient himself. When asked about one of the wishes that stand out in his mind, he didn't hesitate and mentioned a Roseberg woman. "She had cancer, and she couldn't afford her medicine," he said. "I read that [on the application] and said, 'Okay, that's ridiculous. We're going to fix that. Let's buy her medicine for as long as she needs it.'"

Nine months later, Davis's assistant came into his office in Roseberg and said a family had come to the bank, and they wanted to see him. "I said, 'What do they want?'" The assistant didn't know, but Davis had them enter his office anyway. "They came in to thank me for improving the quality of their mother's life," he said. "She had passed away. They were crying and hugging me, and I thought, 'Man, this program's good.'"

Yes, it does good, and it's good for business. A true win–win.

TOUGH DECISIONS, RIGHT MOVES: BLACK THURSDAYS SERVE THE GREATER GOOD

Some days just burn themselves into your memory bank—days that hold weight, carry emotional heft, and seem to brand every little detail, from the mundane to the monumental, onto your brain.

On a pleasantly warm, sunny Sunday afternoon in August 2003, in Portland, Oregon, I took my wife; my twelve-year-old son, Toryn; and our seven-year-old daughter, Kathrina, to a barbeque at the home of a friend and work colleague. He had also invited some other friends, including a man I'll call Peter, his wife, and his son, who happened to be twelve years old too. Peter served as a management team leader of Integra Telecom. As Integra Telecom's CEO, I had promoted Peter to this position after he'd successfully moved up the ranks.

I recall watching our sons play together as Peter and I and the other guests enjoyed each other's company, the tasty grilled food, and a couple of Portland's finest locally brewed beers. We chatted about a lot of subjects, mostly those on the lighter side—the upcoming college football season, for which I've long had a passion, our families, summer vacations, hobbies, and from time to time, we talked a little shop, proudly.

And why not? My team and I had been doing quite well, tapping the potential of our workforce and building a company from nine initial employees in 1996 into one that then employed nearly four hundred people and was generating more than $100 million in revenue—pretty good growth in seven short years. At that time, I had no idea that we would grow to attain a market value of nearly $2 billion, rewarding our investors by returning nearly four times their investment. I did know, however, that we had something special in our operating model and emerging culture.

At the time, in that backyard over beers and barbecue, we were confident that, based on the gains we'd made in just seven years, we stood at the cusp of something big, something special. We didn't gloat about our nascent success—we were all too cautious to do that—but we were proud of our progress. We also kept the shoptalk in check, for the most part, so as not to put off the other guests and our spouses. Nothing can dampen a party more quickly than having a few chatty office mates prattle on about work.

One of the things I noticed most about that day was just how well Peter's son and Toryn got along. They really hit it off. Our wives enjoyed each other, too, and I considered Peter a good friend. He was easy to like, given that he's articulate, charismatic, friendly, and loyal to the company. In his general management position, he was responsible for many employees, dozens of which reported directly to him. He played a very important role; he held a big-time job.

At one point during the party, I remember looking at Peter as he told a story, laughing with the other guests, soaking up the sunshine, exhibiting his dry and often self-deprecating humor. He seemed so happy. I also recall my mood that day. I found myself focusing in momentarily and then drifting out of conversations. Sometimes I'd feel my gut wrench as I watched Peter, his wife, and his son. They were a very lovely family, I thought.

But I couldn't enjoy their enjoyment of the day, nor much of the day itself, really, because I knew that, later that week, I'd turn their lives upside down. On Thursday, I would fire my friend. I knew that the next four days would be excruciatingly painful for me, and then, at the end of the day on Thursday, it'd be even worse for Peter and his family. I wondered how the termination would transpire, how I'd perform this nasty but necessary deed, and how Peter would react. I speculated about what in the world he'd think of me, the guy who had choked off his six-figure income and cut through his career lifeline.

The Productive Power of Passion

Although I didn't know it at the time, the thinking behind my decision to terminate Peter could be classified under the large umbrella of what some call *servant leadership*, which I discussed in the opening pages of this book.

While many tenets provide the foundation for servant leadership—those that embrace morality, share power, show compassion and empathy, exhibit modesty, and employ active listening, among many more—servant leaders place their organization first and foremost and supplicate their own needs so that it will succeed. Put another way, servant leaders make their company's needs their highest priority. They define their job as serving its employees, customers, and stakeholders.

I evolved to view myself as one of those leaders, but I didn't classify myself that way in the summer of 2003, when I came to my decision about Peter.

I thought of the Fusion Leadership label years later, on discovering one fundamental difference between Fusion Leadership and my understanding of servant leadership. My research into servant leadership suggests that the servant leader is required to place his or her ego below that of the organization or the collective ego. As I mentioned in the introduction, I don't think we're wired that way. I believe our actions are inherently self-serving and that placing the collective ego on an *equal* level resonates within an organization and serves the fusion process.

I dedicate significant thought to the ideal of placing others ahead of myself, which (as a Christian) is one of my religion's main teachings. I hope to get to that level in my faith. Yet our world needs a practical leadership model that can be implemented now, that includes all people and harmonizes an organization at every person's level. Of course, I believe that model is Fusion Leadership.

I've seen how passion in the workplace fuels productivity, how it inspires innovation and kick-starts employees' work days, every day. All of the best C-suite leaders, vice presidents, middle managers, supervisors, and frontline employees I've worked with—those who really got things done and found satisfaction from their careers—have been passionate about their jobs. Consequently, as managers and leaders, we should task ourselves with promoting such passion. Your relationships with people stand front and center at the intersection of stellar leadership, members of the team, and productive results. I've come to realize that building trust and showing people you care about who they are as individuals serve as key components in creating, nurturing, and maintaining a passion-driven organization.

Another way to promote passion is to push the selfish ego aside and pull the collective ego into our thoughts, our decisions, our actions.

KNOWING FULL WELL THAT THE AXE MUST FALL

And that gets us back to Peter . . . and me. The knot gnawing deeper into my stomach during that sunny, happy-on-the-surface Sunday barbeque. The impending termination on Black Thursday. Peter's wife. His son. My son. . . . Yikes!

At the picnic, I kept glancing over at the two twelve-year-old boys playing so well together, doing twelve-year-old-boy stuff as if they'd been best buddies for months. As a father, you love to see your son make friends. Yet I was mortified, because here I was at this light-hearted gathering of friends and colleagues and spouses and kids, realizing that I was going to fire Peter that coming week. I was picturing driving home after the picnic and hearing Toryn say, "When can I have a play date with that boy, Daddy? I like him, and I had fun with him." I wasn't sure how I was going to answer that question.

I had promoted Peter to a leadership position because he impressed me as someone who really understood the business. He knew how to drive sales in a way that drove profits. But about a year after promoting him, I began to conclude that I'd made a mistake. In Peter's case, I realized that he really did not have all the skills necessary to succeed in his role, and while the company was doing well, his region lagged behind. I had fired a few people by that point in my career, but this one was especially tough. Peter was a solid performer. He generated results. But I wanted A-level performers. Our fused workforce was performing at a very high standard, and I wanted to set the bar even higher.

Because our close-to-the-customer model required all customer interaction functions to report up to the local market, with full profit and loss responsibility, this was one of the most important jobs in the company. If I was going to improve results, it started with Peter. He had to go. And I hated the situation.

Today's movies and reality shows seem to suggest that my sense of dread differed from how some leaders feel. These honchos are portrayed as relishing the opportunity to exert power, show the underling who's really the boss, have their secretaries draw up termination papers, call in the about-to-be-terminated employee, and hand over the pink slip—in the middle of day, so he or she must walk away in disgrace, for all to see, with tail between legs. Some leaders are sadists who delight in the pain written large across the face of the newly unemployed. I'm tempted to call that a Neanderthal way of behaving, but I wouldn't want to disrespect our distant relatives.

But most people I know who are in the position to make such decisions detest the termination process. I know I do. I know I especially did when it came to Peter, my friend. But this is where Fusion Leadership comes into play. I knew I had to thrust my selfish ego aside for the collective ego, for the good of the organization. All week long, I felt very challenged to put the interests of the company ahead of my desire to have my son be friends with his son. I was struggling with doing what was right for the company at the expense of both a personal friendship and a family relationship that I perceived as valuable. What's more, I was terrified that someday my son would ask me, "Whatever happened to Peter, and what happened to his son?"

To this day, I'll be driving through traffic, and I'll think of Peter's son and that Sunday afternoon and how horrible it was. But I knew I had to deal with this challenge. The company's livelihood was at risk. It was gut-wrenching. I had to do something for the company that was physically upsetting to me. I had not slept well that entire week, and, to this day, I get upset thinking about it.

In the time leading up to my termination meeting with Peter, I never thought that what ended up happening on that Black Thursday would actually happen, that Peter would react in the manner he did. But it did indeed transpire that way, and he did indeed respond the way he did—to my complete and utter surprise.

The Tactics behind Choosing Thursday

At Integra Telecom, I developed a structured process for firing a key employee—it became part of the company's overarching communications philosophy and plan. Termination is a necessary evil, and you can do it coldly or overzealously or matter-of-factly. Or you can do it as humanely as possible, tying in as much of the Fusion Leadership model as possible, which is, of course, how I tried to do it as the company's CEO.

I would work with human resources to draw up a carefully worded but straightforward letter of termination and place it in a manila envelope to be presented to the employee when I delivered the bad news. I always waited until the end of the day so that the person could leave with everyone else, like it was a regular end-of-the-day exit, without having to walk out in the middle of the day in disgrace. I selected Thursday because Saturday is only thirty-six hours away and the former employees could come back then, when the office was empty, to pack up their belongings, if they didn't do it Thursday night.

Then, that gave me Friday, the day after firing someone, to get the word out to the appropriate people. It's very important to control the message as to why the firing occurred. I always met with fired employees' subordinates to let them know what the cause of termination was, and I'd explain who they were now reporting to so they had immediate clarity on their role. I would answer the question about whether they should feel threatened or not threatened because their boss was fired.

As I've suggested, some CEOs—too many, I'm afraid—don't take this approach. In their view, the people who worked with or for the fired employee don't need to know the rationale for the termination. "I'm the boss," these executives seem to think. "It's none of their damn business why Charlie got canned." And that sort of close-to-the-vest attitude and strategy tends to manifest time and time again with these types of leaders. That is, rather than share information, thereby creating and cultivating a culture of transparency, they're likely to hoard and hide information, clinging to it because they think it empowers them.

Those of us who adhere to Fusion Leadership, however, understand that it's imperative to tell anyone whose work relates to the person fired why he or she was let go, because first and foremost, these people have relationships with their supervisor, peer, or colleague. They deserve to know as much as you can disclose about the reasons for the termination, provided you don't violate the fired person's privacy rights. What's more, I find that the first question that comes to mind for employees is, "What does this mean for me, and how will I be treated if I'm ever fired?" So I always try to be very businesslike, very factual, not hiding information, just stating the business reasons for the termination. After all, if I couldn't articulate those reasons, then I wouldn't have just cause to fire that employee.

Usually, I had the replacement person ready to go. I would get that new hire introduced as the new manager as soon as possible to eliminate any gap in authority or accountability. In the case of a higher-up manager, I'd issue a company-wide communiqué to explain what happened, why I did it, and how we were going to move forward. So, by the end of that Friday, it would all be understood. People would come back Monday morning, and we wouldn't miss a beat. We'd conduct our business, serve our customers, and essentially proceed steadfastly down our regular path with a strong sense of continuity firmly rooted within the organization.

Now, I should be clear about something: You can't always roll this way. If someone violated company policy or shared information with the competition or sexually harassed someone, I had to fire them on the spot, no matter what day of the week it was. Think of Ray Davis, in blue jeans, after cutting short his vacation in Washington, DC, to fire Mike. Remember the expedited manner in which I had to fire Bill, as I discussed in chapter 4.

A Study in Contrasts

In Peter's case, as I mentioned, it was a Thursday when I met with him to render his termination letter. Just like the Sunday before at the picnic, that Thursday was—as are many days from July through mid-October in Portland—bright and sunny and stroll-in-the-park beautiful. But I felt no sunshine. I felt like a dark cloud loomed over me. I remember that feeling too well, and, in fact, like at the barbeque, I recall virtually all of the details of that dreadful day.

Finally, as the work day came to a close, I called Peter and asked him to meet me in the conference room of our unglamorous but serviceable building on the west side of town in an unremarkable, low-rise office park. The room was windowless, which perhaps was for the best, because any sunlight streaming in would have only infused unnecessary irony to the bleak task at hand. Peter was dressed casually, a colored polo shirt and khakis, while I wore (unfortunately, I later thought) an expensive suit and tie. I asked him to sit at the long conference table. He took the end-of-the-table chair, and I sat next to him, so we shared the corner of the table together. It was just the two of us, a couple of friends and colleagues—at least for the moment.

He saw the manila envelope on the table, and I think he immediately knew what lay inside it. As directly as I could, I said, "I'm terminating you, Peter, because I don't have the confidence that you can be successful in the role I promoted you into."

He paused a moment, looked me in the eyes, and said, calmly, "I understand, Dudley."

That surprised me a little. But what he said next surprised me a lot—or, rather, it actually shocked me.

"Gee, this must be very hard for you," Peter said empathetically.

I'm sure I was showing how difficult it was, and he picked right up on it. He was such a gracious gentleman to think of *me and my feelings* as I was *firing* him.

His reaction was one of confidence, which I didn't expect. He must have known the extent to which I thought things weren't working out, that they couldn't be rectified, and that his neck was on the line. He likely had thought about what he would do if this day came. He seemed to be somewhat prepared for it.

I, on the other hand, was not at all prepared for it. While my mouth was saying the word *terminating*, my mind was focused on his son. His wife. How he'd tell her. The fear and uncertainty I'd just set in motion. And I couldn't help but think about how I'd be reacting if I were in his shoes. But he was composed, dignified, and considerate enough to ask how I was doing and notice how difficult the task was for me. Unbelievable. I didn't know what to say. I *do* know that this thought flashed like neon through my brain: *Wow, he's a stronger person than I am to have the courage to talk to me in such a gracious manner while I'm firing him.*

I remember having feelings of insecurity, because here he was, dressed casually, acting confident and poised, maintaining an air of—dare I say it—tranquility, and there I was, the armored businessman with the requisite suit and tie, sweat beaded above my brow, anxiety writ across my face.

He stood. I stood. We shook hands. He wished me well, and I followed his lead. And then Peter walked out the door.

A Key Plank in the Fusion Leadership Model

While Peter exhibited empathy with me, I like to think that he realized I, too, was extending the same feelings for him. Mutual empathy is, absolutely, an important tenet of Fusion Leadership. It builds trust. People trust each other when they know that their colleague or manager or CEO cares about their well-being. Employees are constantly asking themselves the question *Am I working for an organization that's looking out for the people, or am I working for one that's only looking out for its own self-interests?*

Peter also knew that he would receive a generous severance package. As I mentioned in the story about closing the Colorado office, I always offered very good severance pay. It's just the right way to treat people, on the one hand. On the other, it makes good business sense. I felt that, because I was tough on people and would fire them for underperformance, our employees knew that, if they underperformed, they could be terminated. But I didn't want them, as they were underperforming, to spend the day on the phone with headhunters looking for their next job. I wanted them to provide every last amount of energy and competency to succeed at their job. The way I tried to communicate this message—that it would be safe for them to work hard and not look for a new job—was to give them generous severance pay.

I was always criticized by my board of directors for this approach. They'd look at the expenses the company incurred when I fired somebody, and they'd say, "You pay more than any other company for this." My response was, "Yes but it's the right thing to do, and we get enormous value for this."

A fused organization—one whose members embrace and exercise reciprocal respect and share common goals for collective success—is poised to rise to the challenge of high expectations, to dare to be the best in its field. From this vantage point, there is no alternative. The Fusion Leader answers the question *Who is going to kick ass—and how will it be done?*

When you fire employees, you send one of the strongest messages possible about your company's values, which is one reason I chose to end the book with this subject. Termination sends the signal that you hold people accountable, that you expect performance and contributions, and that you won't tolerate underperformance. It also conveys how you feel about people. If you fire somebody and simply throw them out on the street with no severance, no safety net, and no ability to take care of their family, many of the remaining employees are going to run for the door and find a better work environment, because that's going to scare the crap out of them.

And, as far as I'm concerned, there's something else: If you don't consider the well-being of others, even as you're giving them the boot—well—good luck looking yourself in the mirror.

HOW DO YOU APPLY THE MANIFESTO FOR A MOVEMENT?

STRIVE TO THRIVE: REFLECTIONS ON THE NEVER-ENDING JOURNEY

What do Pope Francis, the late musician Jerry Garcia of the Grateful Dead, the current singer-superstar Drake, and one of our nation's greatest-ever poets, Robert Frost, have in common? (And like you, no doubt, I've never seen, let alone written, a sentence that includes all four of those very different people.) Give up? Well, they've all reflected on the journey/trip/road of life, and two of them—Garcia and Frost—came to mind when I was reflecting on my journey as a Fusion Leader and on the conclusion of this book. (Full disclosure: I learned about what Pope Francis and Drake said about the journey from a famous-quote Internet search.)

The pope once said, "Life is a journey. When we stop, things don't go right." That observation certainly holds true for Fusion Leadership. Whether you're a CEO or a middle manager or a supervisor, you need to keep pushing forward—sure, rest occasionally—but evolve with an open mind and steady pace, and you'll do a lot to energize your workforce, team, or group.

In one of the Dead's most famous songs, "Truckin'," Garcia sang about the strange lengthy trip he, his band, and, presumably, many of us have taken. When you reflect back on your journey thus far, you do see a lot of head-shaking twists and turns that could be characterized as strange. I know I encountered many surprises as the CEO of Integra Telecom, as well as when I talked to the contributors of this book.

Drake has said, "Sometimes it's the journey that teaches you a lot about your destination." The talented young man is absolutely right. When you make decisions along the way, as you work to achieve success in your endeavor, you discover many things about what that end result actually is.

And then there's the famous line from Frost's poem "The Road Not Taken," in which he wrote about an old decision to take one of two paths in the woods. He took the less-travelled road, and that choice made all the difference. Fusion Leadership doesn't travel down the crowded, familiar leadership highway. This model proceeds differently from most others; the traffic's not heavy, but I'm hoping more and more leaders will take this path—that, of course, is the primary goal of this book.

When I started thinking about writing this book and then researching and interviewing contributors for it, I knew I was embarking on a journey. I also knew I wanted to take readers along with me, primarily because the leaders I talked to share many of those guiding values, which are really an extension of, with a certain twist, the basic principles of leadership: You have to own a vision; you have to be the boss; you have to make the hard decisions; you have to drive the organization. These are traditional themes. The book's contributors and I illustrate these tenets through stories about how we delivered fundamental and important management practices, but in ways that differ from those of many other leaders.

And, as I mentioned, this trek also surprised me at times; I'll discuss both the validations and the surprises later in this conclusion.

First, however, I want to talk about another journey—one that's sweaty, grueling, invigorating, beautiful, and, most importantly, relationship enhancing.

Legging It Up Leg 29

The Hood to Coast Relay attracts thousands of runners every year. While the race—which begins on Oregon's spectacular Mt. Hood and finishes at the Pacific Ocean, on the stunning Oregon Coast—has been a very popular event in the Northwest for years, it's becoming a national event. This annual summer race is for twelve-person teams, and I've run it many times, for many years, with friends, usually college buddies. The thing about this race is that when it's not your turn to run, you spend a lot of time together in the team van with sweaty people, so you don't want to commit to the event unless you're with people you like. The conditions you go through are extreme, as they can start chilly, become very hot, and then eventually end cool and usually windy at the coast. You don't sleep, essentially, for twenty-four-plus hours. You're exerting yourself physically because you have to run every four to five hours. You don't eat much. It really tests your perseverance and your relationships with the other people on your team.

After several years of races, many of my college friends got to the point where their lives were too busy or their knees were too sore for them to continue to participate in Hood to Coast. So a couple of people I'd run with at Integra Telecom suggested that we form our own team. We did that, and, eventually, the company became a sponsor of the race. It was a great opportunity to be with these people who I worked with every day, spending some time away from the office, out in the back woods of Oregon, getting to know each other better.

One of the amazing benefits of Fusion Leadership is that you can nurture collective creativity with a team of people. That can be in the form of problem-solving or, in this case, in the form of playfulness.

The race encompasses thirty-six different segments, or *legs*, and each of the twelve team members runs three times. While each leg is distinctive for various reasons, Leg 29 is—well—legendary, or, if you will, *leg-endary*. Anybody who has ever run this relay or even heard about it knows about Leg 29, because it entails scaling a monster of a hill in the Coast Range of Oregon. The leg is about a five-and-a-half-mile stretch, and, for the first three and a half of these miles, you ascend the hill over a winding narrow road that was built for logging trucks. You climb an elevation gain of many hundreds of feet, so, physically, this is a beast that wants to kick your already-tired ass. If you're the runner for the demanding Leg 29, you've already run one stretch during the previous day and another in the middle of the night, and now you must conquer the ultimate point of exertion—your third and final stint in the heat of the late-August day.

I've run this bad boy, and, let me tell you, I both love it and hate it. The hate part of this mix needs little explanation, other than to say your muscles ache, your chest tightens, your body perspires, and your head pounds. But, even as you're struggling, you know that, soon, you'll crest over the top, leaving the Willamette Valley on one side of the run to enter the coastal area for the last two miles, which is downhill and cooler because you begin to feel the coastal breezes. Running this leg is a transformative experience that shifts you from incredible difficulty and struggle on the way up the front of the hill to astonishing exultation on the way down the back of the hill.

We used to draw straws to see who would run this leg. Jim, who was the oldest and most competitive among us on this Integra Telecom team—and he would probably say the toughest—would always try to angle himself to run this leg.

Jim came up with a great idea that many of us at Integra Telecom built on. He thought, in part because we were a sponsor, that we should post signs so that racers running up the hill and hitting the three-mile mark would start to see placards on posts every two hundred feet or so. They'd see five or six of these signs as they finished the last half-mile of this steepest, most difficult part of the hill. So we *ran* with the idea, if you'll pardon the pun, using the signs as a way to both motivate the runners and promote Integra Telecom's unique service model. One read, *Does your current service provider make you feel the way you're feeling right now?* Another said, *Doesn't it sometimes feel like your telecom provider is an extra load of weight on your back?* Another: *Doesn't it sometimes feel like the way your service provider mistreats you may never end, like this hill is feeling right now?* The signs would acknowledge the enormous pain runners went through as they neared the top.

Exultation on the Summit

But then Leg 29 runners would reach the top and be greeted by a wonderful outpouring of volunteers from our company who would be up there playing music and passing out beverages and singing and cheering. In some cases, we would create a makeshift finish line for the leg by stretching a roll of unfurled toilet paper across the road.

We would delight people by recognizing them and congratulating them and celebrating their success of climbing this monstrous slope before they would descend down the cooler, easier backside of the hill, where we'd have more signs. They'd read, *Consider switching to Integra Telecom. Your experience with Integra Telecom will give you the feeling of the wind at your back, like you're experiencing right now.* Or *Switching to Integra Telecom will be nothing but a downhill experience for you compared to what you're used to in the industry.*

Over the next few years, after we launched this idea, we'd come up with different sayings for the signs, and many people came to associate Leg 29 with Integra Telecom.

In the months leading up to each annual Hood to Coast, several of us would spend hours collectively writing these signs and designing this motivational exercise that we would implement on Leg 29—in some ways, *our* Leg 29. The race organizers and the runners loved the signs and the party atmosphere we created at the apex of the killer hill. The whole experience caught on and grew at Integra Telecom, creating a snowball effect. Scores of our employees would take their families out into the woods to gather, cheer, and celebrate as the runners reached the top. It became a beloved annual gathering that bonded our people together and clearly served as a playful but effective, outside the office— *way* outside the office—Fusion tool. And the more non–Integra

Telecom people talked about how cool it was, the prouder we all became of the company and the creative collaboration that made it all happen.

Well, as the years went by, I didn't really think about our time on Leg 29. But, recently, I was talking to someone—not associated with Integra Telecom—and the subject of running came up. The conversation turned to the Hood to Coast Relay. I told him that one of my favorite legs to run was the last one, which finishes at the beach with all the huge crowds and excitement. He told me that his favorite leg was—you guessed it—Leg 29. He started telling me why it was his favorite leg and recalled the experience he went through with these motivational signs and the group of employees at the top of the hill who were passing out water and playing music and dancing in the woods. He didn't know about my involvement until I shared it with him.

It really struck me how remarkable the whole creative process was. It resulted in lasting happy memories for this person and made me wonder how many other people had similar experiences and similar fond recollections.

We as human beings are relationship-driven in our friendships and families. When it comes to work, I have to ask myself, *What's the difference between the relationships you create in the Fusion Leadership model and any other work environment?* I don't have a scientifically precise answer for that question. But I can say that what stands out and what this story illustrates is this: The Fusion Leadership model promotes an environment where respect for one another can flourish and spread and where challenging each other and debating the hard questions is encouraged. I believe that the relationships you form with your work colleagues, whether they're other leaders and managers or frontline employees, hinge on the qualities that bring out the best in people.

That motivational experience in the Coast Range of Oregon in the middle of nowhere produced a unity among Integra Telecom employees at the time and good memories for people, both inside and outside the company. It serves as testament to what the Fusion Leadership model cultivates.

Why Didn't You Write about That?

During my writing journey, many people asked if I would write about the other edge of the selfish-ego sword. What happens when a power leader becomes intoxicated by his or her selfish ego? Hmm. That is tempting, and wow, could I share stories. Stories of devastated and lost organizations. Stories of lost jobs. Stories of lost wealth. Stories of unfortunate social consequences. In the end, however, that is, in a sad sense, a well-traveled path. Consider Worldcom, Enron, and the Philippines under the Marcos family. Yet that is not what this book is about. By focusing on the selfish-ego-versus-collective-ego dilemma, I hope to provide *all* leaders a glimpse into our innate wiring, sharing stories about real people, amazing people, and how we all encounter this struggle—at least at some level. If you know a power leader who is a little intoxicated by his or her ego, give him or her a copy of this book!

What I Learned along the Way

As I mentioned, all of the stories the book's contributors told me offered validation for the values we've built into Fusion Leadership. I'll touch on a few. The former CEO of WOW!, Colleen Abdoulah, for example, talked about one of her days working with a cable installer and hauling around ladders to give her that on-the-ground experience. But more importantly, her stint helped demonstrate to the installer that he mattered to the success of the organization. That reminded me of working the front line with Janet, in Minnesota, a story I shared in chapter 1. This relatively small act of working alongside employees allows people to connect the dots that their job helps advance the common cause, that they're part of the village. It creates what I call a *positive nuclear reaction*, fusing people—CEOs, managers, mail-room employees—together. And that means a lot.

Another tenet of this leadership approach was substantiated by Ray Davis, the CEO of Umpqua Bank, when he recounted having to call a meeting at an inconvenient time to tell his poorly performing management team that "the train was leaving the station" as he took on the persona of the bad guy, the one who intended to kick some ass.

Even though Fusion Leadership is all about mutual respect, you're still the boss. You've got to be the person who owns the vision. You've got to be prepared to take a strong stand and deal swiftly and severely with anybody who's not embracing the vision. I've certainly had to do things like that. My chapter about firing Peter demonstrates one example of when I had to play the role of the bad guy. Reflecting back, I also realize that perhaps I allowed myself to get too close to Peter and his family. I had to put the corporation and the importance of our vision first. Of course, as the boss, you must find a balance between creating a respectful culture and being the boss. Ray reminded me of the importance of being able to navigate both.

One of the stories that still leaves me scratching my head a little is the narrative Darrell Cavens, of Zulily, shared. He talked about the soft-spoken woman who always hesitated to offer her input on company matters. He asked her to think about how to solve a process design problem overnight, and she came back with an idea that ended up altering the way the company operates. He also told the story about his performance review when he was a younger person and his supervisor figuratively smashed him over his head and said, "If you would just shut up and listen, you'd be a much more effective person." And that changed his behavior; he worked to tamp down his tendency to prove he was the guy with all the answers, all the time.

Now, here's the head-scratcher: Early in this book, I made reference to the story of the senior technical officer Tom and how I used to cut him off at board meetings because, if someone asked him a question, his explanation would include detail after unnecessary detail. I was trying to get him to say the answer that the investors wanted. It prompted one of my team members to pound on my desk and ask me, "What were you doing to Tom?!" That's when the light went on for me. I then had to train myself to refrain from showing off my intelligence by dominating conversations. But, as much as I learned from that experience, I still struggle with that one. Occasionally, I find myself needing to vigorously prove my point, even when I get into an intellectual debate with my wife. She'll often say, "You always need to be right." So I still have more work to do on this.

The idea of Fusion Leadership and its implementation is an endless pursuit. And it's not easy! Even if you grasp the principles intellectually, putting them into practice can often be a struggle, because your selfish ego matters and gets involved. The selfish ego needs to be fed and cared for. Sometimes, if you feed your selfish ego, you forget, and you can compromise the collective ego. This personal process of not always showing how smart I am falls into the work-in-progress category.

Didn't See That Coming

The biggest surprise I encountered involved compensation. I started my journey as a Fusion Leader with the philosophy that you need to pay yourself at a level that's relatively close to the next-highest-compensated person. The message that you're sending is *My economic worth is not materially different from the economic worth of other people in the company.* I assumed this approach would be motivating to people, because it's a very tangible way to communicate a culture of mutual self-worth.

When I discovered, through public information I researched, that one of the leaders I interviewed for the book was compensated at a rate of about three times the next-highest person, my jaw dropped. It was a shock to me, because this person has also built a very successful company and instills a great deal of passion in the company's workforce. I would describe them as a Fusion Leader who has done very good things for our society. And this person is becoming a much wealthier person than I am. I would love to be a fly on the wall in a room where there's a discussion between this leader's direct reports and how they view the leader's compensation. Would this be discouraging to them, or are they okay with it? Might this issue put a bit of a wedge between the other leaders and the CEO and prevent them from soaring to as high a level as they might have, had the boss's compensation been more equitable? My instincts say the leader has at least partially impaired the fusion process because of the inequity in pay. But maybe I'm wrong. Maybe there's no issue at all here.

Another surprise came with the story by Chip Bergh, of Levi Strauss & Co., and how he purposefully declined to take the corner office when he was with Procter & Gamble. This decision was about taking a vision that succeeded in the United States and transferring it to Singapore, with its myriad of different nationalities and cultures. The way he attempted to transfer the vision was, in part, through an open floor plan and a seating arrangement where nobody had offices and everybody had shared workstations.

That reminded me of the story I recounted about rejecting the corner office in the company Integra Telecom acquired in Minneapolis. Here's the difference: When I flew home to Portland, I went back to my corner office. It was modest in size and furnishings, and the artwork consisted of finger paintings that my children made in school. At the time, I felt that these modest accommodations communicated to the employees that I didn't consider myself significantly better than anyone else.

But I have to say Integra Telecom was nowhere near the size of Gillette, which Procter & Gamble acquired, or the Asian operations of P&G, and I didn't have anywhere near the scope of responsibility that Chip had. But he never sat in a corner office. After talking with Chip, I found myself walking away from those discussions asking myself if maybe the selfish ego was a little bit sneakier than I thought it was. Maybe my selfish ego found a way to insert itself in a way that I didn't realize at the time. I now wonder, if I were to do it all over again, if I might go more in the direction in which Chip went.

Yes, Fusion Leadership is a journey. The road is lined with distractions and temptations that arise with money and power. The ultimate destination—a place where the collective ego exists above or at least equal to your selfish ego—is difficult to attain, and I was not always successful. But the rewards we and the other contributors realized by taking steps toward serving the collective ego are undeniable. The high-functioning team at Integra Telecom transformed the telecommunications services industry and enhanced our communities, which generated deep and genuine on-the-job fulfillment and enormous personal success. There's nothing more professionally rewarding. It's the ultimate prize.

Finally, as I mentioned in the introduction, it's my sincere hope that this book inspires leaders to help the members of their organizations satisfy a universal desire to find real meaning in their jobs. When this occurs, we're able to tap into one of the strongest forces on the planet: the power of a committed workforce with a common passion. May the ideas set forth in these pages serve as a manifesto for a movement to enhance workplace satisfaction, increase productivity to meet the many challenges that, collectively, we face—and change the way the world works.

INDEX

ABOUT THE AUTHORS

DUDLEY R. SLATER

Dudley Slater learned firsthand how to inspire and lead people. He cofounded Integra Telecom, Inc. and served as its CEO for fifteen years, growing the company from nine to over 2,000 employees and transitioning it from a start-up to national prominence as one of the ten largest fiber-based telecommunications companies in the United States, generating over $600 million in revenue. Attributing his company's success to its people, Slater became fascinated by the behavioral traits of leaders who successfully create companies that defy national norms and surveys that indicate some 70 percent of US workers hate their job and find little meaning in their work. Partnering with other leaders of iconic, nationally recognized organizations, Slater refined his knowledge and techniques to create the practical, everyday tenets of Fusion Leadership.

Slater architected Integra's growth strategy, targeting business customers with a unique and well-differentiated customer experience, managed with proprietary IT systems and delivered over a best-in-class fiber optic network. Slater handpicked the executive team that executed his competitive strategy, catapulting Integra to national prominence. When Slater retired as CEO in 2011, two thirds of the senior team he assembled in 2000 remained in senior executive positions. *The Oregonian* described the stability of Integra's leadership as "remarkable" when viewed in the context of the "meltdown" that ravaged the telecom industry during the two recessions that marked that period.

Under Slater's leadership, Integra raised over $1.3 billion in capital (bank debt, bonds, and private equity) and constructed one of the most advanced metropolitan fiber networks in its region. At the time Slater transitioned leadership, nearly one in five businesses across eleven states had become an Integra customer, embracing Integra's network and unique, locally staffed service model. *Xchange* magazine described his service model as "a study in the high touch approach" to business customers. Integra was recognized regularly by *Inc.* magazine and the *Portland Business Journal* as one of the fastest-growing companies in Oregon and the United States. The *Portland Business Journal* also cited Integra as one of "Oregon's 10 Most Admired Companies" over six consecutive years from 2005 through 2010.

Slater presently serves or has recently served in a variety of governance, operating, and entrepreneurial roles working with institutional investors and operating companies in the telecommunications, healthcare, banking, and media industries. In addition to his board roles with Umpqua Bank (NASD: UMPQ), WOW! Cable & Internet, and Integra Telecom Inc., Slater's corporate governance and board memberships also include the nation's largest video networking and enterprise collaboration integrator and a super-regional fiber network operator serving enterprise customers in the eastern United States.

His recent operating roles include those as president of one of the nation's largest investors in healthcare technology and alternative healthcare distribution companies and as president and CEO of the largest operator of institutional review boards serving the clinical trials industry. He also serves as an Industrial Advisor to European alternative investment fund EQT. Slater has been a member of the World President Organization (WPO/YPO) for nearly twenty years. Ernst & Young recognized Slater as "Entrepreneur of the Year" in the Northwest in 2011. He earned a bachelor of science in geophysics from UCLA and a master's degree in business administration from the Harvard Business School. Slater has two beautiful grown children (Toryn and Kathrina) and lives with his wife of twenty-nine years, Laurie, in Portland, Oregon, and New York, New York.

STEVEN T. TAYLOR

Steven T. Taylor is an award-winning journalist and writer who's had more than 775 articles, editorials, essays, and other works published by more than sixty organizations and publications, including *The Nation, The Washington Post, Washington City Paper, The Washington Times,* CBS News, *The National Jurist, Public Citizen, Cascadia Times, Willamette Week, Environmental Protection News, Environmental Protection Magazine, E: The Environ-mental Magazine, Technology Transfer Business, Of Counsel, ABA's Law Practice,* and *American City & County.*

He wrote the articles on the environment and the majority of the stories on civil rights and national political events for the best-selling history book *Chronicle of the 20th Century,* which was an American Booksellers Association Book of the Year. He was also a contributor to the best-selling *Chronicle of America.* He received the Washington Press Foundation Award and several journalism grants from various organizations, including the Center for Public Integrity, Voice of the Environment, and the National Forest Accountability Alliance.

Formerly an adjunct professor of journalism at American University, Steve is currently a full professor at the Oregon College of Art and Craft, where he's taught nonfiction writing and public presentation since the fall of 1996. He's also a performance artist and humorist who explores socio-political issues in a medium he's coined "journalistic theater." In this format, performed as hour- to hour-and-a-half-long monologues, he likes to push his concepts to the outer edge—and sometimes beyond.

Steve has two children he's very proud of (college-aged Perry and teenager Julia) and lives with his wife of twenty-two years and best friend, Cindy, in Portland, Oregon.